AUSTIN WHITE—CHICAGO, ILL.—1918

AUSTIN WHITE—CHICAGO, ILL.—1945

This is the last time I want to write my name here.

————————————

[INSCRIPTION DISCOVERED BY A *YANK* REPORTER
ON A WALL OF THE FORTRESS OF VERDUN, FRANCE]

WWII

A Tribute in Art and Literature

EDITED BY DAVID COLBERT

FOREWORD BY JAMES BRADLEY

A FAIR STREET/WELCOME BOOK

TIME
LIFE
BOOKS

CONTENTS

Back Him Up by Thomas Hart Benton, c. 1944. © T. H. Benton and R. P. Benton Testamentary Trusts/Licensed by VAGA, NY.

FOREWORD

HOW FORTUNATE YOU ARE to be holding this book in your hands. How I wish it had been available to me when I started my research on the Second World War.

If you desire to read a single volume that captures the human dimension of history's greatest conflict, this is your book. Or perhaps you are searching for one work that will launch you on a quest to read hundreds of sources; this is for you also.

Not a mere chronology or bloodless retelling of distant history, David Colbert's book presents war at its most emotional, up close and personal. Mr. Colbert has tirelessly scoured books, magazines, newspapers, and the museums and archives of the English-speaking world to bring us this masterful composite of wartime experience. Here you will live WW II through its participants—ordinary people, who had to steel themselves for slaughter and death and, having survived, then had to heal themselves to feel and love again.

Collected stories about WW II exist elsewhere. There are some fine books of photography and military art on the subject. But I know of no other book that pairs vivid and moving literary accounts with superb artistic renderings of the war. If a picture is worth a thousand words, this deeply evocative marriage of words and pictures may well be worth a thousand books.

Through skillful selection of extracts and anecdotes, Mr. Colbert has succeeded in distilling the essence of each author's personal experience. Turn to Primo Levi and descend with him into the horror of Auschwitz; hit the beach at Normandy with a frightened Andy Rooney; feel the sun burn your back as you build a South Pacific airstrip with master storyteller James Michener. Experience the full range of emotions that was WW II as you sing with Irving Berlin, chuckle with Bill Mauldin, and cry with John Hersey. Other books give you an overview; this one gives you the human view.

Here is a book that fulfills the promise of its title. Turn these pages and you will enjoy individual works of "art" and "literature" that collectively form a worthy and thought-provoking "tribute" to the Second World War. Embracing the homefront as well as the battlefront, *WWII: A Tribute in Art and Literature* is a must for any student of that terrible and wonderful time.

—JAMES BRADLEY

Two Soldiers by Bernard Arnest.

INTRODUCTION

No living soul looking at us, seeing us come bustling ashore to stare in awe at the hollow-eyed, vacant-faced, mean-looking First Marines, could have believed that in three months from that day we would be known as the famed Twenty-fifth Infantry.

—JAMES JONES, author of *From Here to Eternity* and *A Thin Red Line*

"THE WORLD BREAKS EVERYONE and afterwards many are strong at the broken places," Ernest Hemingway wrote in *A Farewell to Arms*, his novel of the First World War. That sentiment sums up what happens to soldiers in every conflict. Although the men who fought in the Second World War have been called the "Greatest Generation," they didn't start out great. The heroes celebrated in books and films were mere mortals whose beliefs and expectations were first dashed and then rebuilt.

This book traces that process. It follows the intimate thoughts and feelings of individuals through what James Jones called "the evolution of a soldier." Every soldier, he said, "must make a compact with himself or with Fate that he is lost. Only then can he function as he ought to function, under fire. He knows and accepts beforehand that he's dead, although he may still be walking around for a while. That soldier you have walking around there with this awareness in him is the final end product of the evolution of a soldier." After the first rush of enthusiasm the reality of war sets in, and the soldier or sailor slowly relinquishes individuality to become part of a vast, industrialized killing machine. Surprisingly, despite having renounced his humanity to survive in the system, he later discovers those human impulses are stronger than ever.

Though this process is elemental to any war, in the Second World War it was particularly easy to lose one's sense of self. The spectacle of the mammoth effort left no one unmoved. As both creator and destroyer, humankind surpassed anything conceived before the war. Participants in the First World War just two decades earlier had been astonished by the appearance of tanks and planes and zeppelins; but that rudimentary machinery was far surpassed by the V-2 rockets, jets, radar, and other tools—including the atomic bomb—of the Second. It was difficult for soldiers and those at home to be sure of their importance in a world that made them feel so small, and which often reduced them and their foes to mere targets on a map thousands of miles away. One of the best-known books of the war took its title, *They Were Expendable*, from this very apprehension.

So what did the men do? What they were ordered to do, of course, because most of the time that meant surviving one more day. With a lot of cynical complaining, and the awareness that things were probably worse for someone else at that very moment, they muddled through long periods of boredom punctuated by moments of absurdity or horror. But something unexpected happened while these men gave themselves over to a larger cause: Innumerable instances of humanity testified to the survival of the individual. Since the war effort regulated most aspects of life, what was left was all the more important. Chance meetings were a humane counterpoint to the commotion. Deep friendships grew—even among people who knew they might not see each other again after the conclusion of a weekend pass.

BOTH POETRY AND FICTION appear here alongside eyewitness accounts. Many of the writers and artists whose works were selected for this book served in the armed forces, including authors Jones, Norman Mailer, and Irwin Shaw, and artists Thomas Hart Benton and Jacob Lawrence. All of them understood that the people they portrayed had been asked to give themselves over to something that might cost them their lives. But not all the pieces in this book are by or about soldiers. There are other voices: women on the home front, who were briefly emancipated; leaders like Winston Churchill and Eleanor Roosevelt; and comedians and songwriters like Bob Hope and Irving Berlin, who provided the lighter moments of the era. The war changed their lives, too. You'll also find the work of poets and scientists and children of soldiers, who consider what this war means for the generations that have followed.

A final thought: Throughout this book you'll encounter individuals who faced the war with doubts. Should I fight? Will I survive? But very few people asked, Why me? That's why we've called it a tribute.

From *A Pacific Sketchbook* by George M. Harding
(Captain in the Marine Corps Reserves), 1943–44.

1. ESPRIT DE CORPS

WHEN THE DOORS of American recruiting centers opened the morning after Pearl Harbor—hours before Congress would meet to declare a state of war—men of every age were already standing in long lines. Oddly, many did not respect the armed forces they were joining. Veterans of the First World War had been poorly treated on their return. Many younger men considered career officers too lazy for civilian life. Some Americans had been staunch isolationists ever since the war in Europe began. But for the volunteers, patriotism was stronger than ambivalence.

And though they constantly wisecracked about GI life, a deep pride grew. As Bill Mauldin, the famous *Yank* cartoonist, recalled, "During the three years I spent in the 45th Division, I was certain that it was not only the best division in the army, but that it *was* the army. Since then I have kicked around in more than fifteen other divisions, and I have found that the men in each of them are convinced that theirs is the best and the only division. That's good. *Esprit* is the thing that holds armies together."

The propaganda effort regularly relayed (and in some cases concocted) tales of esprit back to the home front. Probably the most succinct of them—which also had the virtue of being true—occurred toward the end of the war. In late 1944, when it seemed just a matter of time before the retreating German army would submit to the advancing Allies, a final German offensive surprised the Allies and trapped many troops. During the Battle of the Bulge that

The difficult we do immediately. The impossible takes a little longer.

—SLOGAN OF THE U.S. ARMY CORPS OF ENGINEERS

F6F "Hellcat" pilots pose after shooting down 17 of 20 Japanese planes heading for Tarawa, USS Lexington, November 1943.
Photo by CDR Edward Steichen (Navy).

followed, the troops of General Anthony Clement McAuliffe became hopelessly surrounded. The Germans sent emissaries to offer terms of surrender, but McAuliffe barked a one-word retort that strained the translation skill of the messengers: "Nuts." His answer was radioed across Europe, and his men held out until relief arrived. That's esprit.

One did not need to be in the corps to feel esprit de corps; it held civilians together, too. The Allies in Europe, who had already been fighting for more than two years by the time Pearl Harbor was bombed, learned that lesson during the Battle of Britain and the evacuation from Dunkirk—campaigns in which the heroism of the troops was matched by the gallantry of citizens. And though esprit de corps came slowly to some, as did the firepower needed to back it up, it was a start.

THE UNDERGROUND

LANGSTON HUGHES

Men at War by Jacob Lawrence, 1947.
Collection of the Butler Institute
of American Art, Youngstown, OH.

*In 1939 and 1940, the German army was unstoppable.
Its blitzkrieg through Europe flattened the little opposition
it met. And by then the Japanese were already
entrenched in Manchuria and other Asian territories.
Almost as soon as invading armies arrived, however,
underground resistance forces were formed. At the time,
the United States was officially neutral, and many
Americans wanted to keep the country isolated. Poet
Langston Hughes was among those whose compassion
extended beyond the safety of distance.*

[TO THE ANTI-FASCISTS OF THE OCCUPIED
COUNTRIES OF EUROPE AND ASIA]

Still you bring us with our hands bound,
Our teeth knocked out, our heads broken,
Still you bring us shouting curses,
Or crying, or silent as tomorrow,
Still you bring us to the guillotine,
The shooting wall, the headsman's block.
Or the mass grave in the long trench.

But you can't kill all of us!
You can't silence all of us!
You can't stop all of us!
From Norway to Slovakia, Manchuria to Greece,
We are like those rivers
That fill with the melted snow in spring
And flood the land in all directions.

Our spring will come.

The pent up snows of all the brutal years
Are melting beneath the rising sun of freedom.
The rivers of the world
Will be flooded with strength
And you will be washed away—
You murderers of the people—
You Nazis, Fascists, headsmen,
Appeasers, liars, Quislings,
You will be washed away,
And the land will be fresh and clean again,
Denuded of the past—
For time will give us
Our spring
At last.

The Little Ships

from *The Miracle of Dunkirk*

WALTER LORD

The invading German army smashed through Allied defenses, reaching the English Channel by May 19, 1940. The British Expeditionary Force, and some French troops, retreated toward Dunkirk. Hundreds of thousands of men waited on the beaches. "Nothing but a miracle could save the BEF now, and the end cannot be far off," wrote British General Alan Brooke on May 23. The government mustered more than 220 naval ships to attempt a rescue, but morale remained low. Britain's prime minister Winston Churchill believed only 45,000 troops could be saved. Then a miracle was made to happen.

LIEUTENANT IAN COX, First Lieutenant of the destroyer *Malcolm,* could hardly believe his eyes. There, coming over the horizon toward him, was a mass of dots that filled the sea. The *Malcolm* was bringing her third load of troops back to Dover. The dots were all heading the other way—toward Dunkirk. It was Thursday evening, the 30th of May.

As he watched, the dots materialized into vessels. Here and there were respectable steamers, like the Portsmouth–Isle of Wight car ferry, but mostly they were little ships of every conceivable type—fishing smacks . . . drifters . . . excursion boats . . . glittering white yachts . . . mud-spattered hoppers . . .

open motor launches . . . tugs towing ship's lifeboats . . . Thames sailing barges with their distinctive brown sails . . . cabin cruisers, their bright work gleaming . . . dredges, trawlers, and rust-streaked scows . . . the Admiral Superintendent's barge from Portsmouth with its fancy tassels and ropework.

Cox felt a sudden surge of pride. Being here was no longer just a duty; it was an honor and a privilege. Turning to a somewhat startled chief boatswain's mate standing beside him, he burst into the Saint Crispin's Day passage from Shakespeare's *Henri V:*

> And Gentlemen in England,
>   now abed
> Shall think themselves accurs'd they
>   were not here.

The efforts of the Small Vessels Pool and the Ministry of Shipping were at last paying off. The trickle of little ships that began in Tough's boatyard was turning into a deluge. There was still no public announcement of the evacuation, but England is a small place. In one way or another, the word reached those who were needed.

It was a midnight phone call from the Admiralty that alerted Basil A. Smith, a London accountant and owner of the 24-foot cabin cruiser *Constant Nymph.* Would Smith confirm that his boat was ready for sea and could sail on four hours' notice? Early next morning, May 27, the summons came: take her down to Sheerness at once.

Captain Lemon Webb was nursing the Ipswich spritsailing barge *Tollesbury* up the Thames on an ordinary cargo run. Then a

LEFT:
Dunkirk Beaches
by Richard Eurich, 1940.
Imperial War Museum, London.

FOLLOWING PAGES:
The Withdrawal from Dunkirk
by Charles Cundall, 1940.
Imperial War Museum, London.

Charles Cundall 1940

motorboat eased alongside, and a naval officer ordered him to a nearby jetty. There a tug took her in tow, and *Tollesbury* was on her way to Sheerness, too.

The crew of the Margate lifeboat *Lord Southborough* were playing darts at their favorite pub when their turn came. A cryptic message said report to the boathouse at once. Within hours they were heading direct for Dunkirk—no stop at Sheerness for them. For Coxswain Edward D. Parker it was almost a family outing. His brother and nephew were in his crew; a son had already gone over with the Margate pilot boat; another son was one of Commander Clouston's men on the mole.

The cockle boat fleet of Leigh-on-Sea lay peacefully at anchor on May 30 when the call came for them. Bearing imposing names like *Defender, Endeavour, Resolute,* and *Renown,* they sounded like dreadnoughts; actually they were only 40 feet long with a 2 1/2-foot draft. Normally they were engaged in the humblest of tasks—gathering in the cockle shellfish found in the mud flats of the Thames estuary. The crew were all civilians, but every man volunteered. Seventeen-year-old Ken Horner was considered too young and left behind, but he wasn't about to buy that. He ran home, got his mother's permission, and bicycled off in pursuit of the fleet. He caught up with his boat at Southend.

These vessels came with their crews, but that did not always happen. In the race against time, yachts were often commandeered before their owners could be located. Other weekend sailors just couldn't drop everything and sign up in the Navy for a month—the standard requirement. As the little ships converged on Sheerness and Ramsgate, the main staging points, Admiral Preston's Small Vessels Pool looked around for substitute crews.

Shipwright A. W. Elliott was working in Johnson & Jago's boatyard at Leigh-on-Sea when a bobby pedaled up on a bicycle. He announced that volunteers were needed to get "some chaps" off the French coast. Elliott needed no urging.

... EACH LITTLE SHIP had its own tale of troubles, but at the start they all suffered from one common problem: none of them were armed. Lieutenant C. D. Richards carefully hoarded his stockpile of 105 Lewis machine guns, doling them out only to the tugs and escort vessels.

Later the crews would scavenge the beaches, gathering a plentiful supply of discarded Bren guns; and sometimes a BEF gunner might even attach himself to a vessel, but at first they were defenseless. It was enough to make a member of the crew feel a bit uneasy. "Even a record of the *1812 Overture* would be better than nothing," observed one skipper.

It was 10:00 p.m., May 29, when the first convoy of little ships set out from Ramsgate on the long trip across the Channel. None of the eight launches in the group had any navigating instruments. Nevertheless, Lieutenant R. H. Irving, skipper of the escorting motorboat *Triton,* was confident. Unlike most, he knew these waters well. Waiting outside Ramsgate breakwater, he shouted to the other ships to close up and follow him. Three of the boats developed engine trouble and had to turn back, but the others stuck to *Triton* and arrived safely off La Panne at dawn.

At 1:00 a.m. on the 30th another convoy left Ramsgate—this time, nineteen launches led by the Belgian ferry *Yser*—and from then on the flow steadily increased. By late afternoon it was hard to tell where one convoy ended and the next began. All that night, and the 31st too, the little ships poured across the Channel.

Return from Dunkirk by Sir Muirhead Bone, 1940. Imperial War Museum, London.

Frequently they passed ships like the *Malcolm* heading back to England. Decks packed with troops, they were a sobering sight. For their part, the men on the returning vessels watched this armada of small craft with mounting excitement and pride. The very names seemed to say "England": *Swallow . . . Royal Thames . . . Moss Rose . . . Norwich Belle . . . Duchess of York . . . Blue Bird . . . Pride of Folkestone . . . Palmerston . . . Skylark . . . Nelson . . . Southend Britannia . . . Lady Haig . . . New Prince of Wales.*

Many of the names also had a personal quality, suggesting that this rescue effort was no mere naval operation; that it was really a family affair: *Grace Darling . . . Boy Bruce . . . Our Maggie . . . Our Lizzie . . . Girl Nancy . . . Handy Billie . . . Willie and Alice Auntie Gus. . . . ✱*

Over 600 "little ships" took part in the rescue. By June 4, nearly 340,000 British, French, and Belgian soldiers had been saved.

Pearl Harbor Banner.

From

FROM HERE TO ETERNITY

JAMES JONES

---

*The attack at Pearl Harbor sank or damaged 18 ships, destroyed more than 150 planes, wounded
1,178, and killed 2,403. The Japanese lost just 29 planes and pilots. At the same time, the Japanese
attacked the Philippines, Guam, Midway, Wake Island, and Hong Kong.
Eleven months earlier, the American ambassador to Japan, Joseph Clark Grew, had sent this warning
to the State Department in Washington, D.C.: "There is a lot of talk around town to the effect that the
Japanese, in case of a break with the United States, are planning to go all out in a surprise mass attack
on Pearl Harbor. I rather guess that the boys in Hawaii are not exactly asleep. . . ."
In this scene from Jones's novel about an army caught napping, the surprise attack has just begun.*

IT WAS A TYPICAL SUNDAY morning breakfast, for the first weekend after payday. At least a third of the Company was not home. Another third was still in bed asleep. But the last third more than made up for the absences in the loudness of their drunken laughter and horseplay and the clashing of cutlery and halfpint milk bottles.

Warden was just going back for seconds on both hotcakes and eggs, with that voracious appetite he always had when he was drunk, when this blast shuddered by under the floor and rattled the cups on the tables and then rolled on off across the quad like a high wave at sea in a storm.

He stopped in the doorway of the KP room and looked back at the messhall. He remembered the picture the rest of his life. It had become very quiet and everybody had stopped eating and looked up at each other.

"Must be doin some dynamitin down to Wheeler Field," somebody said tentatively.

"I heard they was clearin some ground for a new fighter strip," somebody else agreed.

That seemed to satisfy everybody. They went back to their eating. Warden heard a laugh ring out above the hungry gnashings of cutlery on china, as he turned back into the KP room. The tail of the chow line was still moving past the two griddles, and he made a mental note to go behind the cooks' serving table when he bucked the line this time, so as not to make it so obvious.

That was when the second blast came. He could hear it a long way off coming toward them under the ground; then it was there before he could move, rattling the cups and plates in the KP sinks and the rinsing racks; then it was gone and he could hear it going away northeast toward the 21st Infantry's football field. Both the KPs were looking at him.

He reached out to put his plate on the nearest flat surface, holding it carefully in both hands so it would not get broken while he congratulated himself on his presence of mind, and then turned back to the messhall, the KPs still watching him.

24

As there was nothing under the plate, it fell on the floor and crashed in the silence, but nobody heard it because the third groundswell of blast had already reached the PX and was just about to them. It passed under, rattling everything, just as he got back to the NCOs' table.

"This is it," somebody said quite simply.

Warden found that his eyes and Stark's eyes were looking into each other. There was nothing on Stark's face, except the slack relaxed peaceful look of drunkenness, and Warden felt there must not be anything on his either. He pulled his mouth up and showed his teeth in a grin, and Stark's face pulled up his mouth in an identical grin. Their eyes were still looking into each other.

Warden grabbed his coffee cup in one hand and his halfpint of milk in the other and ran out through the messhall screendoor onto the porch. The far door, into the dayroom, was already so crowded he could not have pushed through. He ran down the porch and turned into the corridor that ran through to the street and beat them all outside but for one or two. When he stopped and looked back he saw Pete Karelsen and Chief Choate and Stark were all right behind him. Chief Choate had his plate of hotcakes-and-eggs in his left hand and his fork in the other. He took a big bite. Warden turned back and swallowed some coffee.

Down the street over the trees a big column of black smoke was mushrooming up into the sky. The men behind were crowding out the door and pushing those in front out into the street. Almost everybody had brought his bottle of milk to keep from getting it stolen, and a few had brought their coffee too. From the middle of the street Warden could not see any more than he had seen from the edge, just the same big column of black smoke mushrooming up into the sky from down around Wheeler Field. He took a drink of his coffee and pulled the cap off his milk bottle.

Kamikaze by Dwight Shepler, 1945.

"Gimme some of that coffee," Stark said in a dead voice behind him, and held up his own cup. "Mine was empty."

He turned around to hand him the cup and when he turned back a big tall thin redheaded boy who had not been there before was running down the street toward them, his red hair flapping in his self-induced breeze, and his knees coming up to his chin with every step. He looked like he was about to fall over backwards.

"Whats up, Red?" Warden hollered at him. "Whats happening? Wait a minute! Whats going on?"

The red-headed boy went on running down the street concentratedly, his eyes glaring whitely wildly at them.

"The Japs is bombing Wheeler Field!" he hollered over his shoulder. "The Japs is bombing Wheeler Field! I seen the red circles on the wings!"

He went on running down the middle of the street, and quite suddenly right behind him came a big roaring, getting bigger and bigger; behind the roaring came an airplane, leaping out suddenly over the trees.

Warden, along with the rest of them, watched it coming with his milk bottle still at his lips and the twin red flashes winking out from the nose. It came over and down and up and away and was gone, and the stones in the asphalt pavement at his feet popped up in a long curving line that led up the curb and puffs of dust came up from the grass and a line of cement popped out of the wall to the roof, then back down the wall to the grass and off out across the street again in a big S-shaped curve.

With a belated reflex, the crowd of men swept back in a wave toward the door, after the plane was already gone, and then swept right back out again pushing the ones in front into the street again.

Above the street between the trees Warden could see other planes down near the smoke column. They flashed silver like mirrors. Some of them began suddenly to grow larger. His shin hurt from where a stone out of the pavement had popped him.

"All right, you stupid fucks!" he bellowed. "Get back inside! You want to get your ass shot off?"

. . . "ALL RIGHT, ALL RIGHT, you men. Quiet down. Quiet down. Its only a war. Aint you ever been in a war before?"

The word war had the proper effect. They began to yell at each other to shut up and listen.

"I want every man to go upstairs to his bunk and stay there," Warden said. "Each man report to his squad leader. Squad leaders keep your men together at their bunks until you get orders what to do."

The earth shudders rolling up from Wheeler Field were already a commonplace now. Above it, they heard another plane go roaring machinegun-rattling over.

"The CQ will unlock the rifle racks and every man get his rifle and hang onto it. *But stay inside at your bunks.* This aint no maneuvers. You go runnin around outside you'll get your ass shot off. And you cant do no good anyway. You want to be heroes, you'll get plenty chances later; from now on. You'll probly have Japs right in your laps, by time we get down to beach positions. . . ."

WHEN THEY GOT OUT to the porch, they found a knot of men arguing violently with S/Sgt Malleaux in front of the supplyroom.

"I dont give a damn," Malleaux said. "Thats my orders. I cant issue any live ammo without a signed order from an officer."

"But there aint no goddamned officers, you jerk!" somebody protested angrily.

"Then there aint no live ammo," Malleaux said.

"The officers may not get here till noon!"

"I'm sorry, fellows," Malleaux said. "Thats my orders. Lt Ross give them to me himself. No signed order, no ammo."

"What the fuckin hell is all this?" Warden said.

"He wont let us have any ammo, Top," a man said.

"He's got it locked up and the keys in his pocket," another one said.

"Gimme them keys," Warden said.

"Thats my orders, Sergeant," Malleaux said, shaking his head. "I got to have a signed order from an officer before I can issue any live ammo to an enlisted man."

Pete Karelsen came out of the kitchen and across the porch wiping his mouth off with the back of his hand. From the screendoor Stark disappeared inside putting a pint bottle back into his hip pocket under his apron.

"What the hells the matter?" Pete asked his two machinegunners happily.

"He wont give us no ammo, Pete," Grenelli said indignantly.

"Well for—Jesus Christ!" Pete said disgustedly.

"Thats my orders, Sergeant," Malleaux said irrefragably.

From the southeast corner of the quad a plane came over firing, the tracers leading irrevocably in under the porch and up the wall as he flashed over, and the knot of men dived for the stairway.

"Fuck your orders!" Warden bawled. "Gimme them goddam keys!"

Malleaux put his hand in his pocket protectively. "I cant do that, Sergeant. I got my orders, from Lt Ross himself."

"Okay," Warden said happily. "Chief, bust the door down." To Malleaux he said, "Get the hell out of the way."

Choate, and Mikeovitch and Grenelli the two machinegunners, got back for a run at the door, the Chief's big bulk towering over the two lightly built machinegunners.

Malleaux stepped in front of the door.

"You cant get by with this, Sergeant," he told Warden.

"Go ahead," Warden grinned happily at the Chief. "Bust it down. He'll get out of the way." Across the quad, there were already two men up on top of the Headquarters Building.

Chief Choate and the two machinegunners launched themselves at the supplyroom door like three blocking backs bearing down on an end. Malleaux stepped out of the way. The door rattled ponderously.

"This is your responsibility, Sergeant," Malleaux said to Warden. "I did my best."

"Okay," Warden said. "I'll see you get a medal."

"Remember I warned you, Sergeant," Malleaux said.

"Get the fuck out of my way," Warden said.

It took three tries to break the wood screws loose enough to let the Yale night lock come open. Warden was the first one in. The two machinegunners were right behind him, Mikeovitch burrowing into a stack of empty belt boxes looking for full ones while Grenelli got his gun lovingly out of the MG rack. There were men up on both the 3rd and 1st Battalion roofs by now, to meet the planes as they came winging back, on first one then the other of the cross legs of their long figure 8.

Warden grabbed a BAR from the rack and passed it out with a full bag of clips. Somebody grabbed it and took off for the roof, and somebody else stepped up to receive one. Warden passed out three of them from the rack, each with a full bag of clips, before he realized what he was doing.

LOOKING DOWN OVER THE WALL, Warden saw Lt Ross standing in the yard looking up

OPPOSITE:
Japanese Kamikaze Lands on American Aircraft Carrier by Achille Beltrame, 1942.

angrily, large bags under his eyes, a field cap on his uncombed head, his pants still unbuttoned, and his shoes untied and his belt unbuckled. He started buttoning his pants without looking down.

"What the hell are you doing up there, Sergeant?" he yelled. "Why arent you down here taking care of the Company? We're going to move out for the beach in less than an hour. Its probably alive with Japs already."

"Its all taken care of," Warden yelled down. "The men are rolling full field packs right now in the squadroom."

"But we've got to get the kitchen and supply ready to move, too, goddam it," Lt Ross yelled up.

"The kitchen is bein pack," Warden yelled down. "I gave Stark the orders and he's doing it now. Should be all ready in fifteen minutes."

"But the supply—" Lt Ross started to yell up.

"They're loading clips and belts for us," Warden yelled down. "All they got to do is carry the water-cooled MGs for the beach out to the trucks and throw in Leva's old field repair kit and they ready to go.

"And," he yelled, "they makin coffee and sandwidges in the kitchen. Everything's all taken care of. Whynt you get a BAR and come on up?"

"There arent any left," Lt Ross yelled up angrily.

"Then get the hell under cover," Warden yelled down as he looked up. "Here they come."

Lt Ross dived under the porch for the supplyroom, as another single came blasting in from the southeast and the roaring umbrella of fire rose from the roofs to engulf it. It seemed impossible that he could fly right through it and come out untouched. But he did.

Right behind him, but flying due north along Waianae Avenue and the Hq Building,

came another plane; and the umbrella swung that way without even letting go of its triggers.

The plane's gastank exploded immediately into flames that engulfed the whole cockpit and the plane veered off down on the right wing, still going at top speed. As the belly and left under-wing came up into view, the blue circle with the white star in it showed plainly in the bright sunlight. Then it was gone, off down through some trees that sheared off the wings, and the fuselage, still going at top speed, exploded into some unlucky married officer's house quarters with everyone watching it.

"That was one of ours!" Reedy Treadwell said in a small still voice. "That was an American plane!"

"Tough," Warden said, without stopping firing at the new double coming in from the northeast. "The son of a bitch dint have no business there."

After the Jap double had flashed past, unscathed, Warden turned back and made another circuit up and down the roof, his eyes screwed up into that strained look of having been slapped in the face that he sometimes got, and that made a man not want to look at him.

"Be careful, you guys," he said. Up the roof. Down the roof. "That last one was one of ours. Try and be careful. Try and get a look at them before you shoot. Them stupid bastards from Wheeler liable to fly right over here. So try and be careful after this." Up the roof. Down the roof. The same strained squint was in his voice as was in his eyes.

"Sergeant Warden!" Lt Ross roared up from down below. "God damn it! Sergeant *Warden!*"

He ran back to the roof edge. "What now?"

"I want you back down here, god damn it!" Lt Ross yelled up. He had his belt buckled and his shoes tied now and was smoothing back his hair with his fingers under his cap. "I want you to help me get this orderly room ready to move out! You have no business up there! Come down!"

"Goddam it, I'm busy!" Warden yelled. "Get Rosenberry. Theres a goddam war on, Lieutenant."

"I've just come from Col Delbert," Lt Ross yelled up. "And he has given orders we're to move out as soon as this aerial attack is over."

"G Company's ready to move now," Warden yelled down. "And I'm busy. Tell that goddam Henderson to send up some clips and belts."

Lt Ross ran back under the porch and then ran back out again. This time he had a helmet on.

"I told him," he yelled up.

"And tell Stark to send us up some coffee."

"*God damn it!*" Lt Ross raged up at him. "What is this? A Company picnic? Come down here, Sergeant! I want you! Thats an order! Come down here immediately! You hear me? Thats an order! All Company Commanders have orders from Col Delbert personally to get ready to move out within the hour!"

"Whats that?" Warden yelled. "I cant hear you."

"I said, we're moving out within the hour."

"What?" Warden yelled. "What? Look out," he yelled; "here they come again!"

Lt Ross dove for the supplyroom and the two ammo carriers ducked their heads back down through the hatch.

Warden ran crouching back to Pete's chimney and rested his BAR on the corner and fired a burst at the V of three that flashed past.

"Get that goddam ammo up here!" he roared at them in the hatchway.

"Milt!" Chief Choate yelled. "'Milt Warden! They want you downstairs."

"You cant find me," Warden yelled. "I've gone someplace else."

Chief nodded and relayed it down over the edge. "I cant find him, Lootenant. He's gone off someplace else." He listened dutifully down over the edge and then turned back to Warden. "Lt Ross says tell you we're moving out within the hour," he yelled.

"You cant find me," Warden yelled.

"Here they come!" Grenelli yelled from the tripod.

They did not move out within the hour. It was almost another hour before the attack was all over. And they did not move out until early afternoon three and a half hours after the attack was over. G Company was ready, but it was the only company in the Regiment that was.

Warden stayed up on the roof, by one subterfuge or another, until the attack was over. Lt Ross, it turned out, stayed down in the supplyroom and helped load ammunition. The Regimental fire umbrella claimed one more positive, and two possibles that might have been hit by the 27th and already going down when they passed over the quad. Stark himself, personally, with two of the KPs, brought them up coffee once, and then still later brought up coffee and sandwiches. In gratitude for which, Pete Karelsen let him take over the MG for a while.

After it was all over, and the dead silence which no sound seemed able to penetrate reigned, they all smoked a last cigarette up on the roof and then, dirty-faced, red-eyed, tired happy and let-down, they trooped down reluctantly into the new pandemonium that was just beginning below and went to roll their full field packs. Nobody had even been scratched. But they could not seem to get outside of the car-ringing dead silence. Even the pandemonium of moving out could not penetrate it. . . .

The Japanese Attack of Pearl Harbor by Griffith Baily Coale, 1944.

Pearl Harbor, when they passed it, was a shambles. Wheeler Field had been bad, but Pearl Harbor numbed the brain. Pearl Harbor made a queasiness in the testicles. Wheeler Field was set back quite a ways from the road, but parts of Pearl Harbor were right on the highway. Up till then it had been a big lark, a picnic; they had fired from the roofs and been fired at from the planes and the cooks had served them coffee and sandwiches and the supply detail had brought them up ammo and they had got two or three planes and only one man in the whole Regiment had been hit (with a .50 caliber in the fleshy part of his calf, didnt even hit a bone, he walked up to the dispensary by himself) and he was getting himself a big Purple Heart. Almost everybody had a bottle and they all had been half-drunk anyway when it started and it had all been a sort of super-range-season with live targets to shoot at. The most exciting kind: Men.

But now the bottles were fast wearing off and there was no immediate prospect of getting any more and there were no live targets to shoot at. Now they were thinking. Why, it might be months—even years— before they could get hold of a bottle again! This was a big war.

As the trucks passed through the new, Married NCO Quarters that had been added onto Pearl Harbor recently, women and children and an occasional old man standing in the yards cheered them. The troops rode on through in silence, staring at them dully.

Going through the back streets of town, all along the route, men, women and children stood on porches fences and roofs and cheered them roundly. They waved Winnie Churchill's V-for-Victory sign at them, and held their thumbs up in the air. Young girls threw them kisses. Mothers of young girls, with tears in their eyes, urged their daughters to throw them more kisses.

The troops, looking wistfully at all this ripe young stuff running around loose that they could not get into, and remembering the old days when civilian girls were not allowed—and did not desire—to speak to soldiers on the street in broad daylight let alone at night in a bar, gave them back the old one-finger salute of the clenched fist jabbing the stiff middle finger into the air. . . .

Among the troops in the trucks there was a certain high fervor of defense and patriotism that exploded into a weak feeble cheer in the heavy perpetual wind, as they passed Lt Ross and The Warden who had climbed out of the jeep on the road-shoulder to watch them go past. A few fists were shaken in the air up between the bare truck ribs and Friday Clark, current-rifleman and ex-apprentice-Company-bugler, shook a wildly promising two-finger V-for-Victory sign at Lt Ross from over the tailgate of the last truck as they pulled on away.

This general patriotic enthusiasm lasted about three days.

Lt Ross, standing beside his jeep to watch his men go off to possible maiming and death, certainly off to war that would last a long time, looked at Friday sadly and without acknowledgment from across a great gulf of years [of] pity and superior knowledge, his eyes set in a powerful emotion, a look of great age and fearful responsibility on his face.

1st/Sgt Warden, standing beside his Company Commander and watching his face, wanted to boot his Company Commander hard in the ass. ✶

Constantine Nicholas Closterides and R.A.P., Biloxi Miss, 1945 by Robert Andrew Parker, 1985.

From
TWO
SOLDIERS

WILLIAM FAULKNER

---

*The day after Pete Grier left for Memphis to enlist,
his protective brother chased after him so Pete
wouldn't have to serve alone.*

. . . THE BUS FELLER said it was time to go,
and I got into the bus jest like Pete done, and
we was gone.

I seen all the towns. I seen all of them.
When the bus got to going good, I found out
I was jest about wore out for sleep. But there
was too much I hadn't never saw before. We
run out of Jefferson and run past fields and
woods, then we would run into another
town and out of that un and past fields and
woods again, and then into another town
with stores and gins and water tanks, and we
run along by the railroad for a spell and I seen
the signal arm move, and then I seen the train

and then some more towns, and I was jest about plumb wore out for sleep, but I couldn't resk it. Then Memphis begun. It seemed like, to me, it went on for miles. We would pass a patch of stores and I would think that was sholy it and the bus would even stop. But it wouldn't be Memphis yet and we would go on again past water tanks and smokestacks on top of the mills, and if they was gins and sawmills, I never knowed there was that many and I never seen any that big, and where they got enough cotton and logs to run um I don't know.

Then I seen Memphis. I knowed I was right this time. It was standing up into the air. It looked like about a dozen whole towns bigger than Jefferson was set up on one edge in a field, standing up into the air higher than ara hill in all Yoknapatawpha County. Then we was in it, with the bus stopping ever few feet, it seemed like to me, and cars rushing past on both sides of it and the streets crowded with folks from ever'where in town that day, until I didn't see how there could 'a' been nobody left in Mis'sippi a-tall to even sell me a bus ticket, let alone write out no case histories. Then the bus stopped. It was another bus dee-po, a heap bigger than the one in Jefferson. And I said, "All right. Where do folks join the Army?"

"What?" the bus feller said.

And I said it again, "Where do folks join the Army?"

"Oh," he said. Then he told me how to get there. I was afraid at first I wouldn't ketch on how to do in a town big as Memphis. But I caught on all right. I never had to ask but twice more. Then I was there, and I was durn glad to git out of all them rushing cars and shoving folks and all that racket fer a spell, and I thought, It won't be long now, and I thought how if there was any kind of a crowd there that had done already joined the Army, too, Pete would likely see me before I seen him. And so I walked into the room. And Pete wasn't there.

He wasn't even there. There was a soldier with a big arrerhead on his sleeve, writing, and two fellers standing in front of him, and there was some more folks there, I reckon. It seems to me I remember some more folks there.

I went to the table where the soldier was writing, and I said, "Where's Pete?" and he looked up and I said, "My brother. Pete Grier. Where is he?"

"What?" the soldier said. "Who?"

And I told him again. "He joined the Army yestiddy. He's going to Pearl Harbor. So am I. I want to ketch him. Where you all got him?" Now they were all looking at me, but I never paid them no mind. "Come on," I said. "Where is he?"

The soldier had quit writing. He had both hands spraddled out on the table. "Oh," he said. "You're going, too, hah?"

"Yes," I said. "They got to have wood and water. I can chop it and tote it. Come on. Where's Pete?"

The soldier stood up. "Who let you in here?" he said. "Go on. Beat it."

"Durn that," I said. "You tell me where Pete—"

I be dog if he couldn't move faster than the bus feller even. He never come over the table, he come around it, he was on me almost before I knowed it, so that I jest had time to jump back and whup out my pocketknife and snap it open and hit one lick, and he hollered and jumped back and grabbed one hand with the other and stood there cussing and hollering.

One of the other fellers grabbed me from behind, and I hit at him with the knife, but I couldn't reach him.

Then both of the fellers had me from behind, and then another soldier come out of a door at the back. He had on a belt with a britching strop over one shoulder.

"What the hell is this?" he said.

"That little son cut me with a knife!" the first soldier hollered. When he said that I

33

tried to git at him again, but both them fellers was holding me, two against one, and the soldier with the backing strop said, "Here, here. Put your knife up, feller. None of us are armed. A man don't knife-fight folks that are barehanded." I could begin to hear him then. He sounded jest like Pete talked to me. "Let him go," he said. They let me go. "Now what's all the trouble about?" And I told him. "I see," he said. "And you come up to see if he was all right before he left."

"No," I said. "I came to—"

But he had already turned to where the first soldier was wropping a handkerchief around his hand.

"Have you got him?" he said. The first soldier went back to the table and looked at some papers.

"Here he is," he said. "He enlisted yestiddy. He's in a detachment leaving this morning for Little Rock." He had a watch stropped on his arm. He looked at it. "The train leaves in about fifty minutes. If I know country boys, they're probably all down there at the station right now."

"Get him up here," the one with the backing strop said. "Phone the station. Tell the porter to get him a cab. And you come with me," he said.

It was another office behind that un, with jest a table and some chairs. We set there while the soldier smoked, and it wasn't long; I knowed Pete's feet soon as I heard them. Then the first soldier opened the door and Pete come in. He never had no soldier clothes on. He looked jest like he did when he got on the bus yestiddy morning, except it seemed to me like it was at least a week, so much had happened, and I had done had to do so much traveling. He come in and there he was, looking at me like he hadn't never left home, except that here we was in Memphis, on the way to Pearl Harbor.

"What in durnation are you doing here?" he said.

And I told him, "You got to have wood and water to cook with. I can chop it and tote it for you-all."

"No," Pete said. "You're going back home."

"No, Pete," I said. "I got to go too. I got to. It hurts my heart, Pete."

"No," Pete said. He looked at the soldier. "I jest don't know what could have happened to him, lootenant," he said. "He never drawed a knife on anybody before in his life." He looked at me. "What did you do it for?"

"I don't know," I said. "I jest had to. I jest had to git here. I jest had to find you."

"Well, don't you never do it again, you hear?" Pete said. "You put that knife in your pocket and you keep it there. If I ever again hear of you drawing it on anybody, I'm coming back from wherever I am at and whup the fire out of you. You hear me?"

"I would pure cut a throat if it would bring you back to stay," I said. "Pete," I said. "Pete."

"No," Pete said. Now his voice wasn't hard and quick no more, it was almost quiet, and I knowed now I wouldn't never change him. "You must go home. You must look after maw, and I am depending on you to look after my ten acres. I want you to go back home. Today. Do you hear?"

"I hear," I said.

"Can he get back home by himself?" the soldier said.

"He come up here by himself," Pete said.

"I can get back, I reckon," I said. "I don't live in but one place. I don't reckon it's moved."

Pete taken a dollar out of his pocket and give it to me. "That'll buy your bus ticket right to our mailbox," he said. "I want you to mind the lootenant. He'll send you to the bus. And you go back home and you take care of maw and look after my ten acres and keep that durn knife in your pocket. You hear me?"

"Yes, Pete," I said.

"All right," Pete said. "Now I got to go." He

Poster, United States Army.

put his hand on my head again. But this time he never wrung my neck. He jest laid his hand on my head a minute. And then I be dog if he didn't lean down and kiss me, and I heard his feet and then the door, and I never looked up and that was all, me setting there, rubbing the place where Pete kissed me and the soldier throwed back in his chair, looking out the window and coughing. He reached into his pocket and handed something to me without looking around. It was a piece of chewing gum.

"Much obliged," I said. "Well, I reckon I might as well start back. I got a right fer piece to go."

"Wait," the soldier said. Then he telephoned again and I said again I better start back, and he said again, "Wait. Remember what Pete told you."

So we waited, and then another lady come in, old, too, in a fur coat, too, but she smelled all right, she never had no artermatic writing pen nor no case history neither. She come in and the soldier got up, and she looked around quick until she saw me, and come and put her hand on my shoulder light and quick and easy as maw herself might 'a' done it.

"Come on," she said. "Let's go home to dinner."

"Nome," I said. "I got to ketch the bus to Jefferson."

"I know. There's plenty of time. We'll go home and eat dinner first."

She had a car. And now we was right down in the middle of all them other cars. We was almost under the buses, and all them crowds of people on the street close enough to where I could have talked to them if I had knowed who they was. After a while she stopped the car. "Here we are," she said, and I looked at it, and if all that was her house, she sho had a big family. . . . [W]e went in, and there was another soldier, a old feller, with a britching strop, too, and a silver-colored bird on each shoulder.

"Here we are," the lady said. "This is Colonel McKellogg. Now, what would you like for dinner?"

"I reckon I'll jest have some ham and eggs and coffee," I said.

She had done started to pick up the telephone. She stopped. "Coffee?" she said. "When did you start drinking coffee?"

"I don't know," I said. "I reckon it was before I could remember."

"You're about eight, aren't you?" she said.

"Nome," I said. "I'm eight and ten months. Going on eleven months." ✶

From

THE AIRSTRIP
AT KONORA

from *Tales of the South Pacific*

JAMES MICHENER

The technical limits of Second World War ships and planes required that the Pacific war be fought in small steps, from island to island. The process was arduous: ships and planes would bombard an island's defenses; marines and army troops would land to fight the Japanese; then construction battalions would build whatever was necessary to launch an attack on the next island in the chain.

WHEN ADMIRAL KESTER finally finished studying Alligator operations he said to himself: "They'll be wanting a bomber strip at Konora to do the dirty work." He looked at his maps. Konora was a pinpoint of an island, 320 miles from Kuralei. When you went into Konora, you tipped your hand. Japs would know you were headed somewhere important. But they wouldn't know whether your next step would be Kuralei, Truk, or Kavieng. Therefore, you would have some slight advantage.

But you'd have to move fast! From the first moment you set foot on Konora, you knew the weight of the entire Jap empire would rush to protect the next islands. You couldn't give the enemy much time. When you went into Konora, the chips were down. You batted out an airstrip in record time, or else . . .

At this point in his reasoning Admiral Kester asked me to get Commander Hoag, of the 144 Seabees. Immediately. Soon Commander Hoag appeared. He was a big man, about six foot three, weighed well over 200 pounds, had broad shoulders, long legs, big hands, and bushy eyebrows. He wore his shirt with the top two buttons unfastened, so that he looked sloppy. But a mat of hair, showing on his chest, made you forget that. He was a Georgia man. Had been a contractor in Connecticut before the war. As a small-boat enthusiast, he knew many Navy men. One of them had prevailed upon him to enter the SeaBees. To do so cost him $22,000 a year, for he was a wealthy man in civilian life. Yet he loved the order and discipline of Navy ways. He was forty-seven and had two children.

"Commander Hoag to see you, sir!" I reported.

"So soon?" the admiral asked. "Bring him in."

Hoag loomed into the doorway and stepped briskly to the admiral's desk. "You wished to see me, sir?" I started to go.

"Don't leave," Kester said. "I'll want you to serve as liaison on this job." The admiral made no motion whereby we might be seated, so like schoolboys we stood before his rough desk.

"Hoag," he said briefly. "Can you build a bomber strip on Konora?"

"Yessir!" Hoag replied, his eyes betraying his excitement.

"How do you know?" Kester inquired.

"I've studied every island in this area that could possibly have a bomber strip. Konora would handle one. There are some tough problems, though. We'd have to round up all the Australians and missionaries who'd ever been there. Some tough questions about that island. Maps don't show much."

"Could the strip be completed for action within fifteen days of the minute you get your first trucks ashore?"

Without a moment's hesitation Hoag replied, "Yessir."

"Lay all preparations to do the job, Hoag. D-day will be in five weeks. You'll be the sec-ond echelon. You'll probably not need combat units, since the Marines should reduce the island in two days. But you'd better be prepared. Logistics and Intelligence will give you all the assistance you demand. You can write your own ticket, Hoag. But remember. Tremendous importance accrues to the time table in this operation. Bombers must be ready to land on the sixteenth day."

"They will be," Hoag replied in a grim voice that came deep from his chest. "You can schedule them now."

"Very well!" the admiral said. "I will."

I worked with Commander Hoag for the next five weeks. I was his errand boy, and scurried around to steal shipping space, essential tools, and key men. It was decided to throw the 144th and five maintenance units of SeaBees onto Konora. Some would

In the Ready Room by Tom Lea, 1942.

38

build roads; others would knock down the jungle; others would haul coral; some would run electrical plants; important units would do nothing but keep gigantic machinery in operation; one batch of men would build living quarters.

"Coral worries me," Hoag said many times as he studied his maps. "I can't find records anywhere of coral pits on that island. Yet there must be. Damn it all, it would be the only island in that general region that didn't have some. Of course. Somewhere in our push north we're going to hit the island without coral. Then hell pops. But I just can't believe this island is it. One of those hills has got to have some coral. God!" he sighed. "It would be awful if we had to dig it all from sea water. Get those experts in here again!"

When the experts on coral returned, Hoag was standing before a large map of Konora. The island was like a man's leg bent slightly at the knee. It looked something like a boomerang, but the joining knee was not so pronounced. Neither leg was long enough for a bomber strip, which had to be at least 6,000 feet long. But by throwing the strip directly

across the bend, the operation was possible. In this way it would cut across both legs. Since the enclosed angle pointed south, the strip would thus face due east and west. That was good for the winds in the region.

"Now men," Hoag said wearily. "Let's go over this damned thing again. The only place we can possibly build this strip is across the angle. The two legs are out. We all agree on that?" The men assented.

"That gives us two problems. First might be called the problem of the ravine. Lieutenant Pearlstein, have you clarified your reasoning on that?"

Pearlstein, a very big Jewish boy, whom his men loved because of his willingness to raise hell in their behalf, moved to the map. His father had been a builder in New York. "Commander," he said. "I'm morally certain there must be a big ravine running north and south through that elbow. I'm sure of it, but the photographs don't show it. We can't find anyone who has been there. They always landed on the ends of the island. But look at the watershed! It's got to be that way!"

"I don't think so," a young ensign

From *A Pacific Sketchbook* by George M. Harding (Captain in the Marine Corps Reserves), 1943–44.

retorted. It was De Vito, from Columbus, Ohio. He graduated from Michigan and had worked in Detroit. There was a poll of the men. The general opinion was that there was no severe ravine on Konora.

"But commander," Pearlstein argued. "Why not run the strip as far to the north as possible? Cut the length to five thousand feet. If you keep it where you have it now, you'll get the extra length, that's right. But you're going to hit a ravine. I'm certain you will."

Commander Hoag spoke to me. "See if a strip five thousand feet long would be acceptable," he ordered. I made proper inquiries among the air experts and was told that if no longer strip was humanly possible, five thousand would have to do. But an extra thousand feet would save the lives of at least fifteen pilots. I reported this fact.

Everyone looked at Pearlstein. He countered with another proposal. "Then why not drop one end of the strip as far as possible down this east leg? You could still run the other end across the elbow. And you'd be so far north on the elbow that you'd miss the ravine."

"See if they could use a strip like that?" I was told. "Let's see. Wind on takeoff and landing would come from about three hundred and twenty-five degrees."

I soon returned with information that our airmen considered 325 cross wind much less acceptable than earlier plans they had approved. "It's all right for an empty, normal plane," I reported. "But these bombers are going to be loaded to the last stretching ounce."

Hoag stood up. "Plans go ahead as organized. Now as to the coral!" The commander and his officers gathered about the map. With red chalk he marked two hills, one at the northern tip of the elbow and one about halfway up the western leg. He then made many marks along the shoreline that lay within the bend of the knee.

"We can be pretty certain there will be coral here," he reasoned, indicating the shoreline. "But what do you think about these two hills?" His men argued the pros and cons of the hills. In some South Pacific islands SeaBees' work was made relatively easy by the discovery of some small mountain of solid coral. Then all they had to do was bulldoze the wonderful sea rock loose, pile it onto trucks, haul it to where it was needed, and smash it flat with a roller. The result was a road, or a path, or a dock, or an airstrip that almost matched cement. But on other islands, like Guadalcanal and Bougainville, for example, there was no coral, either in mountains or along the bays. Then the SeaBees swore and sweated, and for as long as Americans lived on those islands, they would eat lava dust, have it in their beds at night, and watch it disappear from their roads with every rain. If, as some Navy men have suggested, the country ought to build a monument to the SeaBees, the SeaBees should, in turn, build a monument to Coral. It was their stanchest ally.

"The Australians are here, sir," a messenger announced.

Two long, thin men and one woman, old and un-pretty, stepped into the room. Commander Hoag gave the tired woman his chair. The men remained standing. They introduced themselves as Mr. and Mrs. Wilkins and Mr. Heskwith. Eighteen years ago they had lived on Konora for three months. They were the only people we could find who knew the island.

It was quiet in the hot room as these three outposts of empire endeavored to recall the scene of one of their many defeats in the islands. They had made no money there. The mosquitoes were unbearable. Trading boats refused to put into the lagoon. The natives

FOLLOWING PAGES:
Detail from *RAAF Kittyhawk Squadron at Milne Bay, New Guinea* by William Dargie, 1969. Australian War Memorial, Canberra.

42

were unfriendly. Mr. Heskwith lost his wife on Konora. He had never remarried. Even though we were rushed, no one interrupted the dismal narrative.

The Wilkinses and Mr. Heskwith had then gone to Guadalcanal. We wondered what had been the subtle arrangements between Mr. Heskwith and Mrs. Wilkins. Faded, in an ill-fitting dress, she seemed scarcely the magnet that would hold two men to her thatched hut for eighteen years. "At Guadalcanal we were doing nicely," Mr. Wilkins concluded, "when the Japanese came. We saw them burn our place to the ground. We were up in the hills. My wife and I were some of the first to greet the American troops. Mr. Heskwith, you see, was scouting with the native boys. He met your men later. Mr. Heskwith has been recommended for a medal of some kind by your naval forces. He was of great service to your cause."

Gaunt Mr. Heskwith smiled in a sickly manner. We wondered what he could have done to help the United States Navy.

"Very well," Commander Hoag said. "We are proud to have you people and Mr. Heskwith here to help us again. You understand that you will be virtual prisoners for the next four or five weeks. We are going to invade Konora shortly and are going to build a bomber strip across the bend. Just as you see it on this map. We dare not risk any idle conversation about it. You'll be under guard till we land."

"Of course," Mr. Wilkins said. "We were the other time, too."

The three Australians then studied the map in silence. We were abashed when Mrs. Wilkins dryly observed, "I didn't know the island looked like that." We looked at one another.

"Now point out where you lived," Commander Hoag suggested.

"It was here," Mr. Wilkins said, making an X on the map.

"No," his wife corrected. "I'm sorry, David, but it was over here." They could not even agree as to which leg of the island they had settled on.

"Could you take the map down from the wall?" Mr. Wilkins asked. "It might be easier to recall." Commander Hoag and one of his officers untacked the large map and placed it on the floor. "That's better!" Mr. Wilkins said brightly. He and his wife walked around the map, squinted at it, held their heads on one side. They could not agree. Mr. Wilkins even found it difficult to believe that north was north.

"See!" Commander Hoag said quietly. "It's the same on other maps. That's north." Still the Wilkinses could not determine where they had lived. "But try to think!" Hoag suggested. "Which way did the sun rise?"

"They asked us that in the other room, sir," Mrs. Wilkins explained. "But we can't remember. It's been so long ago. And we wouldn't want to tell you anything that wasn't true."

"Mr. Heskwith!" Hoag said suddenly. "Perhaps you could tell us something." The thin fellow was studying the western leg of the island. "Do you recall something now?" Hoag asked.

"I'm trying to find where it was we buried Marie," the man replied. "It was not far from a bay."

Hoag stepped aside as the three middle-aged people tried to recall even the slightest certainty about that far and unhappy chapter of their lives. No agreement was reached. No agreement could be reached. Time had dimmed the events. It was all right for people to say, "I can see it as plain as if it was yesterday." But some things, fortunately, do not remain as clear as they were yesterday. The mind obliterates them, as Konora had been obliterated.

"May I ask a question, sir?" Lieutenant Pearlstein suggested. When the commander assented, he took the three Australians to the head of the map. "Now it would be very helpful if you could tell us something definite about this bend here. You see the airstrip has to pass right over it. Were any of you ever in that region?"

All three volunteered to speak, but by consent granted eighteen years before, Mr. Wilkins acted as chairman. "Yes," he said. "That's the logical place to settle. We went there first, didn't we? But we didn't like it."

"But why didn't you?" Pearlstein asked triumphantly.

"No breeze," Wilkins said briefly. Pearlstein's smile vanished.

"Did you ever go inland at this point?" he continued.

"Come to the question, Pearlstein," Hoag interrupted impatiently. "What we need to know," he said in a kindly manner, "is whether or not there is a deep ravine across the bend?"

The Australians looked at one another blankly. Mutually, they began to shake their heads. "We wouldn't know that, sir," Mr. Wilkins said.

"The only person likely to know that," Mrs. Wilkins added, "is Mr. Davenport."

"Who's Davenport?" Hoag demanded with some excitement.

"He's the New Zealander who lived on the island for about a dozen years," Mrs. Wilkins explained.

"Why didn't we get Davenport up here?" Hoag demanded.

"Oh!" Mrs. Wilkins explained. "The Japs caught him. And all his family."

Hoag was stumped. He spoke with Pearlstein a few minutes while the Australians studied the large map of the tiny island. Pearlstein returned to the map. "Can you think of anyone who might know about that bend?" he asked. "You can see how urgent it is that we satisfy our minds as to that ravine." The Australians wrinkled their brows.

"No," Mr. Wilkins said aloud. "The skipper of the *Alceste* wouldn't be likely to know that."

"Not likely," Mrs. Wilkins agreed.

It was Mr. Heskwith who had the bright idea! He stepped forward hesitatingly. "Why don't you send one of us back to the island?" he suggested.

"Yes!" the Wilkinses agreed. They all stepped a few paces forward, toward Commander Hoag. He was taken aback by the proposal.

"There are Japs on the island. Hundreds of them," he said roughly.

"We know!" Mrs. Wilkins replied.

"You think you could make it?" Pearlstein asked.

"We could try," Mr. Wilkins said. It was as if he had volunteered to go to the corner for groceries.

"You have submarines to do things like that, don't you?" Mrs. Wilkins asked.

"Do you mean that you three would go up there?" Commander Hoag asked, incredulously.

"Yes," Mr. Wilkins replied, establishing himself as the authority.

"I think I should go," Mr. Heskwith reasoned.

"He has been in the woods more," Mrs. Wilkins agreed. "Maybe three of us should go by different routes."

Commander Hoag thought a minute. He stepped to the map. "Is either of these mountains coral?" he asked.

"We don't know," Mr. Wilkins answered.

"Pearlstein! Could a man tell if a mountain was coral? How far would he have to dig?"

"I should say . . . Well, five feet, sir. In three different places. That's a minimum sample."

Commander Hoag turned to Mr. Heskwith. "Would you be willing to risk it?" he asked.

44

"Of course," Heskwith replied. It was agreed upon.

I was given the job of selecting from volunteers ten enlisted men to make the trip. All one hot afternoon I sat in a little office and watched the faces of brave men who were willing to risk the landing on Konora. There was no clue to their coming, no pattern which directed these particular men to apply. I saw forty-odd men that day and would have been glad to lead any of them on a landing party.

They had but one thing in common. Each man, as he came in to see me, fingered his hat and looked foolish. Almost all of them said something like: "I hear you got a job," or "What's this about a job?" I have since learned that when the Japs want volunteers for something unduly risky, their officers rise and shout at the men about ancestors, emperors, and glory. In the SeaBees, at least, you sort of pass the word around, and pretty soon forty guys come ambling in with their hats in their hands, nervous like.

Married men I rejected, although I did not doubt that some of them had ample reason to want to try their luck on Konora. Very young boys I turned down, too. The first man I accepted was Luther Billis, who knew native tongues and who was born to die on some island like Konora. The gold ring in his left ear danced as he mumbled something about liking to have a kid named Hyman go along. I told him to get Hyman. A thin Jewish boy, scared to death, appeared. I accepted him, too. The other eight were average unimpressive American young men. It would be fashionable, I suppose, to say that I had selected ten of America's "little people" for an adventure against the Japs. But when a fellow crawls ashore on Konora at night to dig three holes five feet deep, he's not "little people." He's damned big, brother!

As soon as the group was dispatched, Commander Hoag and his staff seemingly forgot all about them. Mr. and Mrs. Wilkins

were sent back to Intelligence. In their place Admiral Kester's leading aviation assistants were called in. Commander Hoag was tough with them.

"I want plenty of air cover on this job," he said briskly as I took notes. "And I want it to be air cover. No stunting around. I don't want the men distracted by a lot of wild men up in the air. And under no circumstances are your men to attempt landings on the airstrip until I give the word." The aviators smiled at one another.

"An aviator's no good if he's not tough," one of them observed.

"Right! Same goes for SeaBees. But tell them to save their stuff for the Nips. Now what do you think of this? You men are the doctors. Tell me if it's possible. Let's have a constant patrol of New Zealanders in P-40s for low cover. They like those heavy planes and do a good clean-up job with them. Give us some F6Fs or F4Us for high cover. And send some TBFs out every morning, noon, and night at least two hundred miles."

"You'll tip your hand, commander," an aviator observed.

"You're right. But the Nips will know we're on the move the minute we hit Konora. Can't help it. So here's what we'll do! We'll send the TBFs in three directions, Kuralei, Truk, Rabaul."

Problems of air cover were settled. Then logistics men appeared and said what ships we could have and when. Oil tankers were dispatched from San Diego to make rendezvous three weeks later. Commissary men discussed problems of food, and gradually the armada formed. On the day we finished preparations, eighteen bombers plastered Konora. The island was under fire from then on. It knew no respite. And from all parts of the Pacific Japan rushed what aid it could. Those Jap officers who had smugly advised against building a fighter strip at Konora—since it would never be attacked—kept their mouths shut and wondered.

Back from Rabaul (RNZAF Corsair Fighters on Torokina Strip, Empress Augusta Bay, Bougainville)
by Russell Clark, 1944. National Collection of War Art, NZ.

Finally Commander Hoag's staff moved its equipment and maps on board a liberty ship. That night, as we mulled over our plans, Mr. Heskwith and Luther Billis returned from their expedition. Billis was resplendent in tattoos and bracelets. He looked fine in the ship's swaying light. Mr. Heskwith was thin, rumpled, reticent.

"We had no trouble," the Australian said quietly. "It was most uneventful."

"Was there a ravine?" Lieutenant Pearlstein asked eagerly.

"A deep one," Mr. Heskwith replied. "Runs due north and south. Two small streams filter into it."

"How deep? At this point?" Hoag demanded.

Mr. Heskwith deferred to Billis. The jangling SeaBee stepped forward and grinned. "Not more than twenty feet," he said.

"And how wide?"

"Thirty yards, maybe," Billis answered. He looked at the Australian.

"Not more," Mr. Heskwith agreed.

"And the two mountains?" Hoag inquired.

"The hills?" Heskwith repeated. "We could not get to that one. We don't know. We were able to dig only one hole on this one. It was late."

"But was it coral?"

"Yes."

Billis interrupted. "We got coral, but it was deeper down than any hills around here. Lots."

"But it was coral?"

"Yes, sir!"

Commander Hoag thanked the men and dismissed them. He smiled when he saw Billis clap a huge hand over Mr. Heskwith's frail shoulder. He heard Billis whispering: "'Guess we told them what they wanted to know, eh, buddy?" ✷

Poster, United States Army.

SOLDIERS *without guns*

From
GONE TO SOLDIERS

MARGE PIERCY

The war created new opportunities for women. They were relied upon more than ever and allowed greater freedom and responsibility than they had enjoyed previously.

Even the armed services depended on women. The army created the WAAC (Women's Army Auxiliary Corps—later shortened to Women's Army Corps), in which almost 100,000 women served between 1942 and 1945. (Formally chartered by Congress in 1948, it lasted another 30 years until women began to enlist in the regular army.) In 1943, a famous female pilot, Jackie Cochran, following the lead of Britain's Royal Air Force, won American approval for training fliers known as WASPs: Women's Airforce Service Pilots.

The navy's branch had a name that seemed dull and bureaucratic at first glance—Women Accepted for Voluntary Emergency Service—but which shortened neatly into the acronym WAVES.

EVERY MONDAY, every Wednesday and every Friday, Bernice hopped on her Schwinn bicycle at seven-thirty A.M. and set off in rain or sun or unseasonable flurries of late snow for the local airport, hoping that the weather would permit her to take off on time. She carried with her an old leather jacket of Jeff's—the plane of course was not heated— her lunch and a small plastic bottle with a funnel, into which she urinated and which she hid in her empty lunch bucket when she landed. She had no idea how other pilots managed, for she had worked out that method herself.

Bernice had never before considered herself especially fortunate to live in central Massachusetts rather than on the coast, but now she did. Women were not allowed to fly for the Civil Air Patrol over the coastal zone, as that was considered dangerous because of U-boats. The Civil Air Patrol officially looked askance at women flying for it at all. When Bernice had joined she had been sternly informed that only auxiliary functions were open to women, running the offices. She had almost given up, during weeks of typing and filing, but the need for pilots was great and Bernice had at least as much experience as most of the pilots flying for the Civil Air Patrol. She had persisted till now she flew regularly for them.

Sometime around the end of April or the middle of May she would finally log in two hundred hours' flying time. She wanted that commercial license more than ever, but she did not have the money. The Civil Air Patrol volunteers were unpaid, and now she had much less time to type faculty papers. If she could finally earn her instructor's license, she might be hired by the War Service Training Program, which taught flying to students. They had kicked women students out of the program, but they still used women instructors.

Even if flying for the Civil Air Patrol was keeping her penniless, she had three days a week of bliss, and if The Professor was cranky about his supper on those nights, she had the excuse of rationing. Moreover, he could not fault her volunteering for the war effort.

What was hard was to return when she was supposed to, after flying her route inspecting power lines against sabotage and forested areas for fires. She felt an urge strong as she supposed the mating instinct was in deer or dogs, to continue, to fly on until she reached the far unknown ocean. She had an intimate view of the little wrinkled hills of her home, of the broad Connecticut, of the hawks migrating north and the flights of small birds, of the farmlands standing under their puddles, of the rain clouds massing over the Berkshires, of the updrafts around Mount Tom. For three days every week she was ecstatic and useful, at one with the fabric body that extended her own. She did not think there had been a time since the death of her mother, when she had been happy for three days of every week.

Sometimes she was called on other days to act as a courier for documents or chemicals or plasma, to impersonate an enemy bomber in an air raid, twice to search for a downed military plane. Her life had a purpose. She begged off the Sunday movies with Mrs. Augustine, for she needed to catch up with housework and the typing that could pay for her commercial license eventually, but not at all any longer impossibly. She had the same schedule that had used to pad out seven days now crammed into the remaining four. Above all she had three days of doing what she was born to do, three days when she put on the little plane like a flimsy extended body, insectlike around her, beautiful as a dragonfly although jeweled only to her, and burst into flight. ✳

FOLLOWING PAGES:
**Detail from *A Balloon Site, Coventry*
by Dame Laura Knight, 1940.
Imperial War Museum, London.**

THE POSTER WAR

Copywriters and artists elevated propaganda posters to high art. The subjects varied widely, but a few themes were sounded repeatedly.

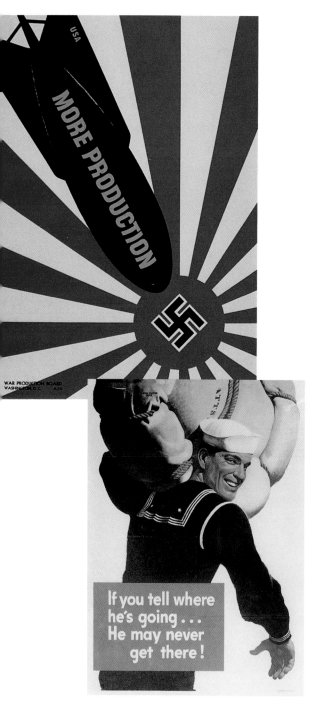

HE'S WATCHING YOU

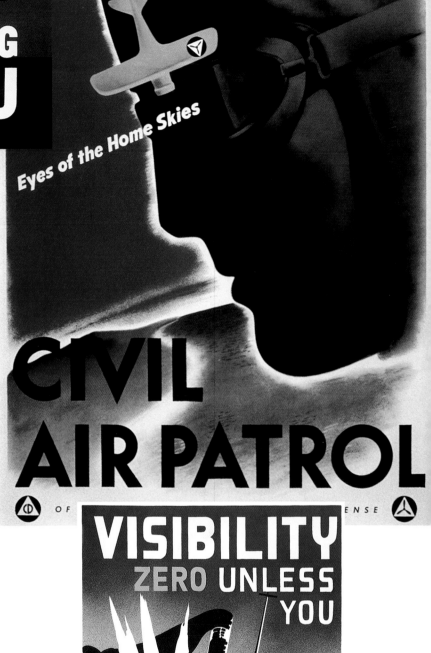

Eyes of the Home Skies

CIVIL AIR PATROL

OF   ENSE

WAAC

THIS IS MY WAR TOO!
WOMEN'S ARMY AUXILIARY CORPS
UNITED · STATES · ARMY

VISIBILITY ZERO UNLESS YOU

LEND YOUR BINOCULARS TO THE NAVY
6 x 30 OR 7 x 50 ZEISS OR BAUSCH AND LOMB
PACK CAREFULLY AND SEND TO NAVY OBSERVATORY
WASHINGTON D.C.

52

*The unspeakable depression of lighting the fires
every morning with papers of a year ago, and
getting glimpses of optimistic headlines as they go
up in smoke.*

—GEORGE ORWELL, diary, 19 October, 1940

Women factory workers in California with transparent
noses for deadly A-20 attack bombers, October 1942.
Photo by Alfred Palmer, 1942.

II. RITUAL

ANY DRILL SERGEANT CAN TELL YOU there are two phases to basic training: first destroy the individual, then rebuild him as part of a unit. Often deliberately irrational, it is madness with a method. As James Jones recalled, "The training, the discipline, the daily humiliations, the privileges of 'brutish' sergeants, the living en masse like schools of fish, are all directed toward breaking down the sense of the sanctity of the physical person, and toward hardening the awareness that a soldier is . . . as dispensable as the ships and guns and tanks and ammo he himself serves and dispenses."

After those six weeks of basic, more madness. No doubt everyone who lived during the Second World War heard the adage, "There are three ways to do something: the right way, the wrong way, and the army way." Fathers told their sons to just "do it the army way. It's easier." Unfortunately, the army way was often unjust, as Lincoln Kirstein recalls here in "Rank." Who you were—or more precisely, whether you were an officer or an enlisted man—often counted more than whether you were right. But any lack of fairness simply reinforced the fatalism that kept soldiers in line.

On the home front, domestic rituals of ration books and scrap drives and car pools reinforced austerity, while millions joined mind-numbing assembly lines. Nonetheless, the human mind proved flexible and evasive. It always found a way to express itself. Workers sang to the rhythmic drone of factories. Soldiers may have been trained to trust their officers and foxhole buddies, but they also relied on superstitions. The rituals of war may have destroyed the individual, but the mind developed its own rituals to keep the individual spirit alive.

Marine's Best Friend by Donald Dickson, 1942.
U.S. Marine Corps Museum, Washington, D.C.

NAMING OF PARTS

from *Lessons of the War*

HENRY REED

To-day we have naming of parts. Yesterday,
We had daily cleaning. And to-morrow morning,
We shall have what to do after firing. But to-day,
To-day we have naming of parts. Japonica
Glistens like coral in all of the neighbouring gardens,
        And to-day we have naming of parts.

This is the lower sling swivel. And this
Is the upper sling swivel, whose use you will see,
        When you are given your slings. And this is the piling
                                        swivel,
Which in your case you have not got. The branches
Hold in the gardens their silent, eloquent gestures,
        Which in our case we have not got.

This is the safety-catch, which is always released
With an easy flick of the thumb. And please do not let me
See anyone using his finger. You can do it quite easy
If you have any strength in your thumb. The blossoms
Are fragile and motionless, never letting anyone see
        Any of them using their finger.

And this you can see is the bolt. The purpose of this
Is to open the breech, as you see. We can slide it
Rapidly backwards and forwards: we call this
Easing the spring. And rapidly backwards and forwards
The early bees are assaulting and fumbling the flowers:
        They call it easing the Spring.
They call it easing the Spring: it is perfectly easy
If you have any strength in your thumb: like the bolt,
And the breech, and the cocking-piece, and the point of
                                        balance,
Which in our case we have not got; and the almond-blossom
Silent in all of the gardens and the bees going backwards
                                        and forwards,
        For to-day we have naming of parts.

OPPOSITE:
Poster, War Production Co-ordinating Committee.

FOLLOWING SPREAD:
Convalescent Nurses Making Camouflage Nets by Evelyn Dunbar. Imperial War Museum, London.

ROSIE THE RIVETER

NELL GILES

During the war, five million women worked in jobs previously held by men, and in many other jobs that had never before existed. Giles, a writer for a Boston newspaper, took a job at a war plant to report on the experience.

TODAY OUR TRAINING CLASS was divided into two shifts . . . night and day . . . and put to work on the bench, though what we do is just for practice.

My first job was being taught the value of motions. The foreman sat me down before an arrangement of screws, tiny wires and things called "brackets." With a small "jeweler's screw driver" I was to take fifty of the things apart and then put them together again. Then I was to take them apart for the second time, and on the next assembling I would be timed. Putting them together is supposed to take 36 minutes . . . and can be done by the experts in 23 . . . but it took me 45. Getting them back together again is even worse because the wires get tangled up, and you wouldn't believe a screw driver could slip around so!

Then the foreman assigned me to the ratchet screw driver, which is a wonderful way to let off steam. I was a whiz at that. All you do is exert a little pressure with this "ratchet" which hangs on a spring in front of you, and out pops the screw. It makes a big noise and you feel the house is falling down around your ears and you hope it does! If every home were equipped with a ratchet screw driver, how it would clear the air of verbal steam letting-off!

Every move we make in completing one of these "jobs" has been carefully figured out by the methods department and put on a blue print, which is constantly before us. "With the left hand place new block on table as right hand removes completed block . . ." and so forth, through every move. As far as possible, the duties of each hand are the same, though in opposite directions. You see that there is a rhythm in all this . . . . ✳

Ten Miles to J Camp by William H. Johnson, 1942. Smithsonian American Art Museum, Washington, D.C.

From

GUARD OF HONOR

JAMES GOULD COZZENS

Guard of Honor, *a novel about the Army Air Force,*
was awarded the Pulitzer Prize for Fiction.

THE PERSONNEL ANALYSIS AUDITORIUM, which could seat several hundred, echoed emptily behind eighty or ninety men in the front rows. It was very warm. It seemed warmer because floodlights, hanging from the beams of a half-dozen, great bowstring trusses that supported the hemicylindrical, flattened round of the roof, were turned on. Between the few windows, the dingy, concrete-block walls were decorated with pictorial charts, bold in line and color, having to do with AAF personnel.

On one chart little blue men marched briskly into tubes displayed like veins or arteries, the various times of entrance being indicated by a list of months along the margin. The tubes swept down, approaching each other, joining. Toward the bottom, all merged; and, two years after the first little blue men (pilots) entered, out came: ONE COMBAT GROUP.

Another showed, foreshortened, the picture of a B-17, bombay doors open, bombs tumbling against a ghastly sky filled in letters of flame by the words: *Bombs Away!* Below, was stated starkly: *What it takes—*. Files of rigid scarlet mannequins showed how many men it took in Air Crew, in Operations, in Maintenance, in Transportation, in Administration, in Housekeeping, for just that one bomber.

Much of the wall opposite was covered by a huge graph headed: GROWTH OF THE ARMY AIR FORCES. Square-jawed silhouettes standing at parade rest succeeded each other. They grew from an homunculus four inches high, labeled 1938, to a prodigy thirteen feet high, labeled 1944.

Colonel Ross eyed these charts, which, while not uninteresting, did not interest him at the moment. He sat motionless, his mind troubled, breathing with a sense of weariness and oppression—the heat of this cavernous hall; the hard long day; the dubious, disagreeable job. He had taken another pill before coming in. He attended the far-off ringing in his ears with glum bemusement, for no gain in cheer or assurance could be expected if he diverted thought from himself to the business on hand. He had tried that. As soon as he sat down he had begun dispassionately to look over the assembled personnel of Project zero-dash-three-three-six-dash-three, to judge their temper as a group; and, if he could, to identify what was probably no more than the handful of hardy spirits on whom any organized action must depend. ✶

SWING-
SONG

LOUIS MacNEICE

I'm only a wartime working girl,
The machine shop makes me deaf,
I have no prospects after the war
And my young man is in the R.A.F.
K for Kitty calling P for Prue . . .
Bomb Doors Open . . .
Over to You.

Night after night as he passes by
I wonder what he's gone to bomb
And I fancy in the jabber of the mad machines
That I hear him talking on the intercom.
K for Kitty calling P for Prue . . .
Bomb Doors Open . . .
Over to You.

So there's no one in the world, I sometimes think,
Such a wallflower as I
For I must talk to myself on the ground
While he is talking to his friends in the sky:
K for Kitty calling P for Prue . . .
Bomb Doors Open . . .
Over to You.

Busy Hands by Howard Baer, 1943.

From

THE SKY MAKES ME HATE IT

WILLIAM CHAPPELL

HOW DO YOU FEEL after sixteen months of Army life? I asked myself. Exactly how do you feel? Stop now, I said, before I could begin to answer. You were going to reply without thinking or considering. Why not? I said. I can reply without thinking and without considering; and I can give you three answers. All of them would be correct, though none of them would describe exactly how I feel. Today it is no longer possible to be exact about the way one feels.

I could say —

I feel much better, thank you,

or

I do not feel at all, thank you,

or

I feel quite differently, than you very much.

Don't thank me, I said to myself. You are so ridiculous with words. You do not understand how to handle or present them; and you know, one does not really give question and answer in the mind. Particularly your mind, I said. Your consciousness is never consecutive. You have no real stream of thought; only a slow circular movement that changes form, and is sometimes globular, sometimes

elliptical. It churns round and round; pauses and churns on. Through it, and across it, small flashing things move; passing so rapidly it is difficult to tell what shape they are.

Each one of your separate thoughts has nine hundred and ninety-nine little offshoots, trailing inelegantly out of its small, fecund inside. One thousand births a second, each like a kitten that is drowned before it can open its staring blue eyes.

It is a miracle that you do not appear a kind of cretin to the world; making grunting sounds, lolling your head, and unable to read or spell.

Don't you quite often despair?

Yes, I said. Not so much, however, as I did during my first six months, and when I despair now it is in a different way. Of course, before the war, I did not know how to despair. My life being free, I did not have to think at all. These days I think all the time, and so deeply that I find I am paying no attention to what people are saying to me, though I can feel my face set in an expression of unreal interest as I continue to answer them. It is almost as though it were being done for me by a familiar spirit, so that I might lean back into the warm darkness of my head, and busy myself with the important work of tracking and listening to my thoughts. My mind is altering. Whether it is due to Army life, or whether my mental condition is a general one, a world warmind, I cannot decide. When I first joined the army I could understand my vague, muddled way of thinking. Now, I cannot understand it at all. I might have undergone a very delicate operation, and been given an unused brain, in which to find my way about. I have to learn to know it and to discover how it functions.

I did not alter during my first few months in the army. I could not even change, as most of the recruits did, that is, by losing weight and looking healthier. My body has always been hard and strong, and I was sunburnt all over a deep golden brown. There was nothing to affect me adversely about my surroundings. I was stationed by the coast on the edge of a town where I had friends. It was summer and the weather was hot, and when it is hot I can be more or less contented anywhere. It was later, at the beginning of the winter, when I was moved to another unit, inland, that I became rather unhappy. It was an unhappiness I could cope with, as I could see all the reasons for it. I was unhappy because I was uncomfortable, and nearly always cold; and I disliked sleeping in one hut with twenty-eight other men; and the food was ugly and unappetizing, and I was tired all the time, and had to do mathematics, which I hated.

IT WAS SHORTLY AFTER MY ARRIVAL at the new station that I began, periodically, to undergo a peculiar new mental condition in which I would suddenly feel as though I were no longer myself. I might be drilling or sitting in the crowded Naafi with people talking all round me and the piano playing; or be on guard, alone in a steely night; or just walking by day through the camp; when abruptly, inside my clothes, my body would dissolve, and harden again to a thin glass centre. My glass bones, and my glass flesh, fragile and brittle, would creep away into a central thinness, avoiding all contact with the outer shell of my clothing. My heavy boots would crash like thunder as I moved. Out of my transparent head, I would look down, and see my boots advancing, neatly, one after the other, with the toes turned in a little; but the feet beneath the polished leather had no substance, and though I could still feel the blisters on my heels, I knew that the feet inside the boots were as unsubstantial as the mists that filled the hollows of the country, and made Japanese landscapes round the camp in the early winter mornings. These strange moments occurred frequently for about six or eight months, and then gradually ceased. . . .

This turning inwards of my thoughts cannot be happening only to me. . . .

No one can be genuinely happy at this time. War, as it welds the people of a nation together, makes every life an isolated life. Everyone is lonely. More lonely than they have ever been before in the life of the world. We have all become strangers; and when the war is over we shall have to start learning once more to know each other. The picture I hold, painted on my mind, of people, things and places is the pre-war picture. When I go on leave there is an air of strangeness about everything and everybody, and I cannot fully enjoy the companionship of my friends and my family, for our lives no longer mix. They run for a while parallel; thin, dusky-coloured streams with a narrow space between them. The mind cannot make the stupendous effort needed to bridge the gap; nor can it do anything to stop the running of the stream when it diverges from its place beside the others, and moves off quietly into a deserted country.

The life I lead in the army gives me nothing. My freedom is restricted, my privacy torn, my comfort abolished. New friendships are almost an impossibility, hardly can the first gestures be made before one or the other of the two people involved is moved away and a crowd of strange faces hem each one about. Army life lacks everything, particularly in a static unit. People do not realize it is worse for the spirit to be dreary than endangered; that boredom is more deadly than bombs.

Even in its fighting aspects, the army has none of the terrible beauty of the airman's flight to the stars and his battles in high space. None of the plunging splendour of the sailors' life in the vast steel ships that cut the spreading seas. And army death is sad: a heap of mutilated bodies, littering the scarred earth in ugly anonymity. Yet this life, that is not an individual's life, is making me more of

Sundown on Peleliu by Tom Lea, September 15, 1944.

an individual, driving my thoughts into deeper, rarer places than they have visited before. I wait for them to bring up to the surface of my consciousness the knowledge that my mind desires. Behind the self that goes about my army duties, I am occupied feverishly, searching to find this new mind that is forming somewhere within me.

I hate to think that war can do anything good for me, yet it has reached into me and made my thoughts, which were moving quietly in a known direction, turn on themselves and move another way, inwards this time, listening; and then down to my heart, whispering, at present so quietly that I cannot hear the words. It makes me restless and uncomfortable not to recognize the meaning, or the shape, of those words. I cannot tell if the other eyes I see hide the same turmoil that my calm gaze protects from the people around me. It seems to be such a very personal thing. One cannot talk of it, or explain it, even to one's friends. It has to be understood and explained by oneself to oneself.

This chaos within my head is bringing about a ruin of the brain that will eventually disclose a place where order and comprehension have always existed. The mind is being wrecked to reveal the foundations on which it can be rebuilt in clear and understandable patterns.

So I find that I accept this life. Accept the loss of my home, the collapse of my career, the bomb that injured my mother, the wide scattering and disintegration of the web of friendship I had woven so painstakingly for myself; accept it all with an equanimity that amazes me. I have always had a character chameleon-like in its capacity for adjustment to new surroundings. This is more than adjustment. It is an intense preoccupation with my innermost being that protects me from everything, without making me self-centred or egotistical in the smallest degree. ✶

All Work by Thomas Hart Benton, 1943.

RANK

LINCOLN KIRSTEIN

Differences between rich and poor, king and queen,
Cat and dog, hot and cold, day and night, now and then,
Are less clearly distinct than all those between
Officers and us: enlisted men.

Not by brass may you guess nor their private latrine
Since distinctions obtain in any real well-run war;
It's when off duty, drunk, one acts nice or mean
In a sawdust-strewn bistro-type bar.

Ours was on a short street near the small market square;
Farmers dropped by for some beer or oftener to tease
The Gargantuan bartender Jean-Pierre
About his sweet wife, Marie-Louise.

GI's got the habit who liked French movies or books,
Tried to talk French or were happy to be left alone;
It was our kinda club; we played chess in nooks
With the farmers. We made it our own.

To this haven one night came an officer bold;
Crocked and ugly, he'd had it in five bars before.
A lurid luster glazed his eye which foretold
He'd better stay out of our shut door,

But did not. He barged in, slung his cap on the zinc:
"Dewbelle veesky," knowing well there was little but beer.
Jean-Pierre showed the list of what one could drink:
"What sorta jerk joint you running here?"

Jean-Pierre had wine but no whisky to sell.
Wine loves the soul. Hard liquor hots up bloody fun,
And it's our rule noncommissioned personnel
Must keep by them their piece called a gun.

As well we are taught, enlisted soldiers may never
Ever surrender this piece—M1, carbine, or rifle
With which no mere officer whomsoever
May freely or foolishly trifle.

70

A porcelain stove glowed in its niche, white and warm.
Jean-Pierre made jokes with us French-speaking boys.
Marie-Louise lay warm in bed far from harm;
Upstairs, snored through the ensuing noise.

This captain swilled beer with minimal grace. He began:
"Shit. What you-all are drinkin's not liquor. It's piss."
Two privates (first class) now consider some plan
To avoid what may result from this.

Captain Stearnes is an Old Army joe. Eighteen years
In the ranks, man and boy; bad luck, small promotion;
Without brains or cash, not the cream of careers.
Frustration makes plenty emotion.

"Now, Mac," Stearnes grins (Buster's name is not Mac; it is Jack),
'Toss me your gun an' I'll show you an old army trick;
At forty feet, with one hand, I'll crack that stove, smack."
"Let's not," drawls Jack back, scared of this prick.

"You young punk," Stearnes now storms, growing moody but mean,
"Do you dream I daren't pull my superior rank?"
His hand snatches Jack's light clean bright carbine.
What riddles the roof is no blank.

The rifle is loaded as combat zones ever require.
His arm kicks back without hurt to a porcelain stove.
Steel drilling plaster and plank, thin paths of fire
Plug Marie-Louise sleeping above.

Formal enquiry subsequent to this shootin'
Had truth and justice separately demanded.
Was Stearnes found guilty? You are darned tootin':
Fined, demoted. More: reprimanded.

The charge was not murder, mayhem, mischief malicious,
Yet something worse, and this they brought out time and again:
Clearly criminal and caddishly vicious
Was his: Drinking With Enlisted Men.

I'm serious. It's what the judge Advocate said:
Strict maintenance of rank or our system is sunk.
Stearnes saluted. Jean-Pierre wept his dead.
Jack and I got see-double drunk.

Preliminary Shakedown, New Orleans by Thomas Hart Benton, 1943.

MAGIC PIECES
and
SUPERSTITION

JOHN STEINBECK

Like many established writers, Steinbeck was eager to report on the war from the field. The Pulitzer Prize–winning novelist took a job as a correspondent for the New York Herald-Tribune. *Rather than describing troop movements and battles, he focused on what was revealed in quiet moments.*

MAGIC PIECES

A GREAT MANY SOLDIERS carry with them some small article, some touchstone or lucky piece or symbol which, if they are lucky in battle, takes on an ever-increasing importance. And being lucky in battle means simply not being hurt. The most obvious magic amulets, of course, are the rabbits' feet on sale in nearly all gift stores. St. Christopher medals are carried by Catholics and non-Catholics alike and in many cases are not considered as religious symbols at all, but as simple lucky pieces.

A novelty company in America has brought out a Testament bound in steel covers to be carried in the shirt pocket over the heart, a gruesome little piece of expediency which has faith in neither the metal nor the Testament but hopes that a combination may work. Many of these have been sold to parents of soldiers, but I have never seen one carried. That particular pocket is for cigarettes and those soldiers who carry Testaments, as many

do, carry them in their pants pockets, and they are never considered as lucky pieces.

The magic articles are of all kinds. There will be a smooth stone, an odd-shaped piece of metal, small photographs encased in cellophane. Many soldiers consider pictures of their wives or parents to be almost protectors from danger. One soldier had removed the handles from his Colt .45 and had carved new ones out of Plexiglass from a wrecked airplane. Then he had installed photographs of his children under the Plexiglass so that his children looked out of the handles of his pistol.

Sometimes coins are considered lucky and rings and pins, usually articles which take their quality from some intimacy with people at home, a gift or the symbol of some old emotional experience. One man carries a locket his dead wife wore as a child and another a string of amber beads his mother once made him wear to ward off colds. The beads now ward off danger.

It is interesting that, as time in action goes on, these magics not only become more valuable and dear but become more secret also. And many men make up small rituals to

OPPOSITE:
**Detail from *Mess Deck, No. 3, Corvette Drumheller*
by Thomas Charles Wood (Lieutenant), 1944.
Canadian War Museum, Ottawa.**

cause their amulets to become active. A smooth stone may be rubbed when the tracers are cutting lines about a man's head. One sergeant holds an Indian-head penny in the palm of his left hand and against the stock of his rifle when he fires. He is just about convinced that he cannot miss if he does this. The employment of this kind of magic is much more widespread than is generally known.

As time goes on, and dangers multiply and perhaps there is a narrow escape or so, the amulet not only takes on an increasing importance but actually achieves a kind of personality. It becomes a thing to talk to and rely on. One such lucky piece is a small wooden pig only about an inch long. Its owner, after having tested it over a period of time and in one or two tight places, believes that this little wooden pig can accomplish remarkable things. Thus, in a bombing, he held the pig in his hand and said, "Pig, this one is not for us." And in a shelling, he said, "Pig, you know that the one that gets me, gets you."

But in addition to simply keeping its owner safe from harm, this pig has been known to raise a fog, smooth out a high sea, procure a beefsteak in a restaurant which had not had one for weeks. It is rumored further that this pig in the hands of a previous owner has commuted an execution, cured assorted cases of illness, and been the direct cause of at least one considerable fortune. This pig's owner would not part with him for anything.

The association between a man and his amulet becomes not only very strong but very private. This is partly a fear of being laughed at, but also a feeling grows that to tell about it is to rob it of some of its powers. Also there is the feeling that the magic must not be called on too often. The virtue of the piece is not inexhaustible. It can run down, therefore it is better to use it sparingly and only to call on it when the need is great.

Novelty companies have taken advantage of this almost universal urge toward magic. They turn out lucky rings by the thousands and coins and little figures, but these have never taken hold the way the associational gadgets do.

Whatever the cause of this reliance on magic amulets, in wartime it is so. And the practice is by no means limited to ignorant or superstitious men. It would seem that in times of great danger and great emotional tumult a man has to reach outside himself for help and comfort, and has to have some supra-personal symbol to hold to. It can be anything at all, an old umbrella handle or a religious symbol, but he has to have it. There are times in war when the sharpest emotion is not fear, but loneliness and littleness. And it is during these times that the smooth stone or the Indian-head penny or the wooden pig are not only desirable but essential. Whatever atavism may call them up, they appear and they seem to fill a need. The dark world is not far from us—from any of us. ✳

SUPERSTITION

IT IS A BAD NIGHT in the barracks, such a night as does not happen very often. Nerves are a little thin and no one is sleepy. The tail gunner of the other outfit in the room gets down from his upper bunk and begins rooting about on the floor.

"What's the matter?" the man on the lower bunk asks.

"I lost my medallion," the tail gunner says.

. . . Everyone gets up and looks. They move the double-decker bunk out from the wall. They empty all the shoes. They look behind the steel lockers. They insist that the gunner go through all his pockets. It isn't a good thing for a man to lose his medallion. . . . The uneasiness creeps all through the room. It takes the channel of being funny. They tell jokes; they rag one another. They

Killing Time Enroute to Normandy by Alexander P. Russo, 1944.

ask shoe sizes of one another to outrage their uneasiness. "What size shoes you wear, Brown? I get them if you conk out." The thing runs bitterly through the room.

And then the jokes stop. There are many little things you do when you go out on a mission. You leave the things that are to be sent home if you have an accident. You leave them under your pillow, your photographs and the letter you wrote and your ring. . . . and you don't make up your bunk. That must be left unmade so that you can slip right in when you get back. . . .You go out clean-shaven too, because you are coming back, to keep your date. You project your mind into the future and the things you are going to do then.

In the barracks they tell of presentiments they have heard about. There was the radio man who one morning folded his bedding neatly on his cot and put his pillow on top. And he folded his clothing into a neat parcel and cleared his locker. He had never done anything like that before. And sure enough, he was shot down that day.

The tail gunner still hasn't found his medallion. He has gone through his pockets over and over again. The brutal talk goes on until one voice says, "For God's sake shut up. It's after midnight. We've got to get some sleep."

The lights are turned out. . . .

It is quiet in the room, and then there is a step, and then a great clatter. A new arrival trying to get to his bunk in the dark has stumbled over the gun rack. The room breaks into loud curses. . . . They tell him where he came from and where they hope he will go. It is a fine, noisy outburst, and the tension goes out of the room. The evil thing has gone.

You are conscious, lying in your bunk, of a droning sound that goes on and on. It is the Royal Air Force going out for night bombing again. . . . Hundreds of Lancasters, with hundreds of tons of bombs. And, when they come back, you will go out. . . .

The barrack room is very silent. From a corner comes a light snore. Someone is talking in his sleep. First a sentence mumbled, and then, "Helen, let's go in the Ferris wheel now."

There is secret sound from the far wall, and then a tiny clink of metal. The tail gunner is still feeling through his pockets for his medallion. ✷

THE ISLAND

JAMES DICKEY

Acclaimed poet and author of the novels Deliverance *and* Anilam, *Dickey left Clemson College when the war began to join the Army Air Corps. Trained as a navigator and radar observer, he flew 39 missions for the 418th Night Fighter Squadron in the Pacific.*

A light come from my head
Showed how to give birth to the dead
That they might nourish me.
In a wink of the blinding sea
I woke through the eyes, and beheld
No change, but what had been,
And what cannot be seen
Any place but a burnt-out war:
The engines, the wheels, and the gear
That bring good men to their backs
Nailed down into wooden blocks,
With the sun on their faces through sand,
And polyps a-building the land
Around them of senseless stone.
The coral and I understood
That these could come to no good
Without the care I could give,
And that I, by them, must live.
I clasped every thought in my head
That bloomed from the magical dead,
And seizing a shovel and rake,
Went out by the ocean to take
My own sweet time, and start
To set a dead army apart.
I hammered the coffins together
Of patience and hobnails and lumber,
And gave them names, and hacked
Deep holes where they were stacked.
Each wooden body, I took
In my arms, and singingly shook
With its being, which stood for my own
More and more, as I laid it down.

At the grave's crude, dazzling verge
My true self strained to emerge
From all they could not save
And did not know they could give.
I buried them where they lay
In the brass-bound heat of the day,
A whole army lying down
In animal-lifted sand.
And then with rake and spade
I curried each place I had stood
On their chests and on their faces,
And planted the rows of crosses
Inside the blue wind of the shore.
I hauled more wood to that ground
And a white fence put around
The soldiers lying in waves
In my life-giving graves.
And a painless joy came to me
When the troopships took to the sea,
And left the changed stone free
Of all but my image and me:
Of the tonsured and perilous green
With its great, delighted design
Of utter finality,
Whose glowing workman stood
In the intricate, knee-high wood
In the midst of the sea's blind leagues,
Kicked off his old fatigues,
Saluted the graves by their rank,
Paraded, lamented, and sank
Into the intelligent light,
And danced, unimagined and free,
Like the sun taking place on the sea.

Burial Ground Guards Around a Fire
by Mitchell Jamieson, June 1944.

Coast Guard landing boat, June 6, 1944.
Photo by Robert F. Sargent (Coast Guard).

III. COURAGE

SOME PEOPLE BELIEVED AMERICA'S ENTRY into the Second World War would be as limited and decisive as our short involvement in the First. However, it soon became apparent that the fight would last much longer, and test more severely each person's resolve. Dylan Thomas expressed this during the 1940 bombing of Britain by Germany, when he wrote one of his best-remembered poems, "A Refusal to Mourn the Death, by Fire, of a Child, in London." The poem itself was an act of mourning, of course. But it was also a statement that Britain would not succumb to Germany's efforts to end the war quickly by inducing terror.

At the forefront of many people's thoughts was the nature of courage. Was it the absence of fear, or the acceptance of it? Did each person have only a limited supply of it? Was it necessary, or perhaps dangerous? The answers differed from those offered during World War I. In that war, modern tools such as long-range artillery and poison gas seemed to make individual combat, and the code of honor that sprang from it, obsolete. Modern communications made it possible for a very few men to command all aspects of a battle, magnifying the effects of each decision, often disastrously.

The more intelligent they are, the more they are frightened. The courageous man is the man who forces himself, in spite of his fear, to carry on. Discipline, pride, self-respect, self-confidence, and the love of glory are attributes which will make a man courageous even when he is afraid.

—GENERAL GEORGE S. PATTON, JR.

That war had left many soldiers cynical. As well, between the wars the world had discovered the work of Sigmund Freud. Courage was analyzed minutely. Historian and literary critic Paul Fussell wrote, "Although in the Great War madness among the troops was commonly imputed to the effects of concussion ('shell shock'), in the Second it was more frankly attributed to fear, and in contrast to the expectations of heroic behavior which set the tone of the earlier war, the fact of fear was now squarely to be faced. The result was a whole new literature of fear, implying that terror openly confessed argues no moral disgrace, although failure to control its visible symptoms is reprehensible."

But even the psychoanalysts could not fully explain courage—why it would appear, and when, and in what form. Those answers were deeply personal, as different as every individual was from another.

LEAVING HOME

from Barry Broadfoot's
Six War Years: 1939–1945

ANONYMOUS

Broadfoot, a renowned Canadian writer and editor, collected stories like this one for an oral history of the Second World War.

I LEFT FOR OVERSEAS on November 10, 1943. I guess that's one red circle on the old calendar I'll always remember. When you're twenty, well, what the hell. The thing is, you're only twenty and you've got those pilot wings. Manning pool, ground school, the Piper Cubs, advanced training. Hoo hah! Know what I mean. Telling this I feel like that kid again.

Oshawa isn't all that big a town and then it was smaller, and everybody on the street knew little old Jerry's leave was up, going away to serve the king. Fly the big bombers or *zoooooooooom* [making a diving motion with his hand] a fighter. I'd been home, what was it, twelve days, fourteen.

I didn't seem to have many friends and it seemed most of the guys I knew in school were in the services anyway, so the last time home was just marking time. Walking around the neighbourhood. That was a pretty big deal in the morning. Downtown in the afternoon. The rink if there was a game at night. I might have a few beers with my father in the Legion.

I'm sort of setting the stage. Quite frankly, I was bored. Nothing to do. Nothing to talk about anyway. Do I talk about war, fighting, and have my mother get up from the table and go to her bedroom? That kind of stuff. They knew I was a pilot, and I knew I had three choices. If I went on coastal patrol it would be a piece of cake, just monotonous. Bomber Command and I had a good chance of going for a Burton. Casualties at that time were pretty fierce. And if I was a fighter pilot, glamourous as all get out, I could expect a good chance of seeing them thar Pearly Gates too. So I didn't talk about it.

The day came. Breakfast was as usual, and Dad stayed home. He worked in a department store. My sister worked at the phone company and she gave me a hug and said, °Look after yourself, Buddy, and write Mom and Dad, please. You know how they are." Then she left.

It was an hour until the taxi came at ten. A condemned man, I know what he goes through. We just sat in the parlour and I guess Mom asked me eight times if I'd like a cup of tea. My gear at the door. Coat on the chair, and hat too. I thought I'd better take a look around and see this place, because maybe it would be the last time. My home, you know. I don't think I was being dramatic or anything like that and certainly not heroic. At twenty? Even at that age you can get pretty realistic.

My mother, she was being brave. A bit trembly and you might say erratic, when she'd start a sentence and trail off and go over and spend a couple of minutes picking a couple of dead leaves off a rubber plant. Straightening a picture. Then asking if I wanted a cup of tea. She was wearing those old slippers from the Boer War and a mauve skirt and a sweater, wool, I think, brown, with a patched hole in the right sleeve. You can see, if I was a painter I could paint that room, that scene, the old mom and dad waiting for their son to go off to war.

My father. My dear father. He'd never missed more than five days off work in his life, I suppose. A real workhorse, loved the company and had a pride in his work, selling men's clothing. The first suit he'd pick off the rack, that would be the right one for the customer. There are men like that. And there he was sitting on the piano bench feeling guilty about missing half a day at the store and yet, here was his only son, first born, that sort of thing, and he had this duty. Stay and see him off. We talked fishing and he went into the back room and got out his notebook and there it all was, on April 19, Buddy had caught three trout, a pound, pound two ounces, a pound six. That passed a bit of time. Fishing data. My one big day. Three fish.

Remember that clock in the movie *High Noon*? Gary Cooper. The big clock going tick-tock tick-tock towards noon when the train with the killers on it would come? Same difference. Our grandfather's clock.

Finally it was ten and I stood up and said, "I gotta go." I put on my gaberdine and picked up my hat and fixed it at the hall mirror. You had to get that right angle. That was important. Off we go, into the wild blue yonder, flying high into the sky. Remember the song? Then the taxi beeped. Twice. I turned and hugged Mom and she had her arms tight around my neck, squeezing as hard as her little body could, and her face was in my shoulder and she said, and I'll remember this, she said, "Goodbye my darling son. Goodbye. Goodbye. Our prayers . . ." And then she gave me the Bible. I knew that Bible, it must have been 40 years old. It was the one she had when she came out to this country as a girl to work as a servant in the house of some mill owner in Stratford. That just about finished me there. Just about finished me. . . .

Then it was Dad's turn. He stuck out his hand and said, "Good luck, son," and that's about what I expected. No nonsense. Just good luck. I grabbed him and hugged him

and his eyes were glistening. The old goat. I loved him. I didn't know it until then, but I did. All the shit life had handed out to him, and he'd taken it and come back for more.

I picked up my little bag and said to my mother, "I'll read the guid booook, mither," imitating the Scots way of speech she had. Then I put my foot under the cat's belly and gave a heave. She'd go up in the air about three feet and come down and come over and brush her tail against my leg. She was a Persian and I'd done it a thousand times and I said, "Okay, Mugger, that's the last time you get boosted for a while."

I went out the door and said, "Bye, folks, I love you all to pieces," and got the hell out of there, down the walk, because I wasn't sure how much more I could take.

There was this old Mr. Lake across the street, an old busy-body if there ever was, and there he was, up against his gate and waiting, waving that old cane of his and yelling, "Give the buggers hell, Buddy. Shoot 'em out of the skies," and I had to laugh. I got in and looked back at the house and maybe it was just the skies, grey, November, remember, and I think it would be snowing in an hour or two, and my father and mother at the door, arms around each other as if they were like two old apple trees growing old together, branches wrapped about, and I waved and I could hear a sob. It was me, and I was crying, but it felt as if the tears were coming from everywhere, like out of my eyes and my forehead and my cheeks and as if my whole face was swimming in tears and I was fumbling around for a hankie as we drove away and I remember the cabbie saying, "Let them come, kid. It'll be over in a minute or two. Christ, I've seen guys ten times as tough as you suddenly start to overflow. Just sit back and let 'em come." ✴

FOLLOWING PAGES:
Leaving Home (Odyssey)
by Richard Gibney, 1991. U.S. Marine
Corps Museum, Washington, D.C.

A Refusal to Mourn the Death, by Fire, of a Child, in London

DYLAN THOMAS

From July to October 1940, the British and German air forces fought the Battle of Britain. Part of the German offensive was night bombing of London and other British cities. The Blitz, as it came to be called, terrified the British but did not defeat them. The Germans eventually dropped their plans for a quick invasion, and halted the air war.

Never until the mankind making
Bird beast and flower
Fathering and all humbling darkness
Tells with silence the last light breaking
And the still hour
Is come of the sea tumbling in harness

And I must enter again the round
Zion of the water bead
And the synagogue of the ear of corn
Shall I let pray the shadow of a sound
Or sow my malt seed
In the least valley of sackcloth to mourn

The majesty and burning of the child's death.
I shall not murder
The mankind of her going with a grave truth
Nor blaspheme down the stations of the breath
With any further
Elegy of innocence and youth.

Deep with the first dead lies London's daughter,
Robed in the long friends,
The grains beyond age, the dark veins of her mother,
Secret by the unmourning water
Of the riding Thames.
After the first death, there is no other.

OPPOSITE:
Detail from *Women and Children in the Tube* by Henry Moore, 1940. Imperial War Museum, London.

From
THEY WERE
EXPENDABLE

WILLIAM L. WHITE

White's 1942 bestseller described the efforts of a Patrol Boat (PT boat) squadron in the Philippines to fend off the Japanese advance following the surprise attacks on Pearl Harbor and other U.S. bases. The U.S. was forced to retreat, prompting General Douglas MacArthur's famous slogan, "I shall return."

Japanese Landing Near Vulcan, Rabaul
by Geoffrey Mainwaring, 1970.
Australian War Memorial, Canberra.

87

"YOU DON'T UNDERSTAND," said the young naval officer, "we were expendable." He was very earnest as he lolled on the bunk in the officers' quarters of the torpedo station at Newport, along with the other three officers who had also just got out of the Philippines.

I admitted I didn't understand.

"Well, it's like this. Suppose you're a sergeant machine-gunner, and your army is retreating and the enemy advancing. The captain takes you to a machine gun covering the road. 'You're to stay here and hold this position,' he tells you. 'For how long?' you ask. 'Never mind,' he answers, 'just hold it.'

Then you know you're expendable. In a war, anything can be expendable—money or gasoline or equipment or most usually men. They are expending you and that machine gun to get time. They don't expect to see either one again. They expect you to stay there and spray that road with steel until you're killed or captured, holding up the enemy for a few minutes or even a precious quarter of an hour.

"You know the situation—that those few minutes gained are worth the life of a man to your army. So you don't mind it until you come back here where people waste hours and days and sometimes weeks, when you've seen your friends give their lives to save minutes—"

"Look, never mind about that," said Lieutenant John Bulkeley, the senior officer. "People don't like to hear about that. I've learned that in the week I've been back. . . ." ✷

From OBASAN

JOY KOGAWA

---

*Not long after Pearl Harbor, the governments of the
United States and Canada, fearful that persons of
Japanese descent might help Japan invade North
America, "relocated"–that was the official term–those
living on the West Coast to inland prison camps.
Joy Kogawa, interned as a child, was already a
respected poet before her novel* Obasan *was published
to international acclaim. In this selection, the
narrator has discovered a journal of letters to her
mother from her mother's sister, Emily.*

April 20 [1942].

I HAVE GONE NUMB TODAY. Is all this real?
Where do I begin? First I got my pass and saw
Dan at last. He's going to Schreiber in two
days. I didn't feel a thing when he told me. It
didn't register at all. Maybe I'm crazy. When
I left, I didn't say goodbye either. Now that
I'm home I still can't feel. He was working in
the Baggage—old Horse Show Building.
Showed me his pay check as something he
couldn't believe—$11.75. He's been there an
awfully long time.

After I saw Dan, and delivered some
medicine for Dad, I saw Eiko and Fumi. Eiko
is working as a steno in the Commission
office there, typing all the routine forms. She
sleeps in a partitioned stall—being on the
staff, so to speak. The stall was the former
home of a pair of stallions and boy oh boy
did they leave their odor behind! The whole
place is impregnated with the smell of
ancient manure. Every other day it's swept
with chloride of lime or something but you
can't disguise horse smells, cow, sheep, pig,
rabbit, and goat smells. And is it dusty! The
toilets are just a sheet-metal trough and up
till now they didn't have partitions or seats.
The women complained, so they put in
partitions and a terribly makeshift seat.
Twelve-year-old boys stay with the women
too. The auto show building, where the
Indian exhibits were, houses the new dining
room and kitchens. Seats 3,000. Looks
awfully permanent. Brick stoves—eight of
them—shiny new mugs—very very barracky.
As for the bunks, they were the most tragic
things I saw there. Steel and wooden frames
at three-foot intervals with thin lumpy straw
ticks, bolsters, and three army blankets of
army quality—no sheets unless you brought
your own. These are the "homes" of the
women I saw. They wouldn't let me or any
"Jap females" into the men's building. There
are constables at the doors—"to prevent further propagation of the species," it said in the
newspaper. The bunks were hung with
sheets and blanket, and clothes of every
color—a regular gypsy caravan—all in a
pathetic attempt at privacy—here and there I
saw a child's doll or teddy bear—I saw two
babies lying beside a mother who was too
weary to get up—she had just thrown herself
across the bed. I felt my throat thicken. I
couldn't bear to look on their faces daring me
to be curious or superior because I still lived
outside. They're stripped of all privacy.

Some of the women were making the
best of things, housecleaning around their
stalls. One was scrubbing and scrubbing trying to get rid of the smell, but that wasn't
possible. And then, Nesan, and then, I found
Grandma Nakane there sitting like a little
troll in all that crowd, with her chin on her
chest. At first I couldn't believe it. She didn't

OPPOSITE:
When Can We Go Home?
**by Henry Sugimoto, 1943. Japanese American
National Museum, Los Angeles, CA.**

90

recognize me. She just stared and stared. Then when I knelt down in front of her, she broke down and clung to me and cried and cried and said she'd rather have died than have come to such a place. Aya and Mark were sick when I told them. We all thought they were safe with friends in Saltspring. She has no idea of what's going on and I

think she may not survive. I presumed Grandpa Nakane was in the men's area, but then I learned he was in the Sick Bay. I brought Eiko to meet Grandma but Grandma wouldn't look up. You know how *yasashi* Grandma is. This is too great a shock for her. She whispered to me that I should leave right away before they caught me too—

Topaz WRA Camp at Night by George Matsusaburo Hibi, 1945. Charles G. Young Research Library, UCLA, Los Angeles, CA.

water. The men looked so terribly at loose ends, wandering around the grounds—sticking their noses through the fence watching the golfers. I felt so heavy I almost couldn't keep going. They are going to move the Vancouver women now and shove them into the Pool before sending them to the camps in the ghost towns.

The other day at the Pool, a visitor dropped his key before a stall in the Livestock Building, and he fished for it with a wire and brought to light manure and maggots. He called the nurse and then they moved all the bunks from the stalls and pried up the wooden floors, and it was the most stomach-turning nauseating thing. So they got fumigators and hoses and tried to wash it all away and got most of it into the drains. But maggots are still breeding and turning up here and there, so one woman with more guts than the others told the nurse (white) about it and protested. She replied, "Well, there are worms in the garden, aren't there?" This particular nurse was a Jap-hater of the most virulent sort. She called them "filthy Japs" to their faces and Fumi gave her what for and had a terrible scrap with her, saying, "What do you think we are? Are we cattle? Are we pigs?" You know how Fumi gets.

The night the first bunch of Nisei refused to go to Schreiber the women and children at the Pool milled around in front of their cage, and one very handsome Mountie came with his truncheon and started to hit them and yelled at them to "get the hell back in there." Eiko's blood boiled over. She strode over to him and shouted, "You put that stick down. What do you think you're doing? Do you think these women and children are cows, that you can beat them back?" Eiko was shaking. She's taken it on herself to fight and now she's on the blacklist and reputed to be a troublemaker. ✶

then she wouldn't say any more. Nesan, maybe it's better where you are, even if they think you're an enemy.

Eiko has taken the woes of the confinees on her thin shoulders and she takes so much punishment. Fumi is worried sick about her. The place has got them both down. There are ten showers for 1,500 women. Hot and cold

WHO'S AFRAID OF THE NEW FOCKE-WULF?

JOHN M. BENNETT

*John M. Bennett served in Britain as a B-17 pilot and commander of a
U.S. Eighth Air Force bomb group. Until early 1944, fighter planes
could not escort the bombers all the way to their targets in Germany,
leaving the latter at the mercy of German fighters. As a result
casualties in bomber units were extraordinarily high. A crew member's
life expectancy was five missions less than the 25 missions required by
the Army Air Force for much of the war.*

Dear Father:

THERE IS AN OLD SAYING which goes somewhat like this, "Cowards die many deaths, but a brave man dies but once." If this saying be true, then I am not only a coward myself, but I am fighting this war with a lot of other cowards. A story in the 8th Air Force tells about a group commander who read an over-zealous advertisement in a magazine which asked the question, "Who's afraid of the new Focke-Wulf?" This group commander cut out the advertisement, signed his name to it and pinned it on the bulletin board. After all of the pilots in the group had confessed their fear by signing, the page was mailed back to the U.S. advertiser. We are all afraid and only liars or fools fail to admit it. ✶

From
BOMBER

LEN DEIGHTON

Author Len Deighton, well known for espionage novels, has written deeply researched histories of the war. He has also fictionalized his encyclopedic knowledge in novels such as the one from which this selection comes.

EACH OF *CREAKING DOOR*'S encounters with night fighters had lasted only a few seconds, but between those encounters had come the tension and tiring concentration of one hundred miles of cross-country instrument flying. After he had evaded Beer by the sudden turn to starboard Lambert continued on, nervously examining every quarter of the sky, but soon it was clear that they had escaped from that attack.

Binty Jones said, "Skip, can Jimmy give me a break? I've got a touch of cramp."

"O.K. with you, Jimmy?" Lambert said.

"O.K., Skip."

"Quickly then."

Lambert felt the trim change as first the wireless operator went back to the upper turret and then Binty climbed down from his seat in the roof and moved farther back to the Elsan, just ahead of the tail. Jimmy Grimm, like most of the wireless operators, was a trained air gunner and he enjoyed the view that the turret afforded him. He touched the grips and the turret turned obediently, the machine guns tilting at the merest finger touch. One of the worst aspects of the wireless operator's job was the heated-air outlet that emerged near his seat. Even wearing the minimum of flying kit, Jimmy had become uncomfortably hot. He slipped one side of his helmet off and pressed his face against the ice-cold Perspex of the turret. It was like a long draft of cold beer.

"O.K., Jimmy?"

"O.K., Skip."

Lambert saw the flicker of the navigator's light as his curtain was pushed aside and guessed that Binty had come forward to the cockpit for a moment. Binty cherished a conviction that flying a bomber was little different from driving a motorcycle and he liked to watch Lambert's activities and tried to commit them to memory. He noticed that the altimeter was steadily turning as they lost height. It was the usual procedure to exchange height for speed from the time the enemy coast was crossed on the return journey.

"What about that photoflash, Binty? See if you can push it out, will you?"

"Can someone give me a hand, Skipper?"

"No," said Lambert.

"I'll give a hand, Skipper," offered Cohen.

"O.K.," said Lambert. "See what you can do."

The moonlight that revealed the bombers to the night fighters was also reassuring to an alert bomber crew. Löwenherz was still dancing through the puffy cumulus far behind them over Rotterdam and no one in *Creaking Door* was aware of his existence. Leutnant Beer had been assigned to a southern part of the Ermine sector. In short, there was not an enemy in sight. Over the ocean one would not expect an 8.8-cm. flak gun, but even if by some magic one was there, *Creaking Door* was nearly three thousand feet higher than the effective range of an 8.8-cm. flak gun.

Lambert was relating these facts to himself when a 10.5-cm. shell—with its superior range—burst near *Creaking Door*'s tailplane. It

OPPOSITE:
**Take Off, Interior of a Bomber Aircraft by Dame Laura Knight, 1943.
Imperial War Museum, London.**

FOLLOWING SPREAD:
B24s on Ploesti Raid by Stanley Dersh.

came from the tail; a strangled thump. A giant's belch that rumbled along the metal throat of stringers and formers. Then came the bad breath of cordite and burning, speeding on the wave of displaced air that pushed Lambert forward against the controls, shook the extinguishers loose and sent Kosher's charts to fill the cockpit with fluttering paper. There was a flash of light too. That came from inside the fuselage. It made the screen turn white and blinded Lambert, whose eyes were adjusted to the dark night.

The control column came to meet Lambert's belly and even with all his strength he could not prevent it from coming. *Door*'s nose reared up like a frightened horse and the sound of the motors changed to a new note of anxiety.

"Micky," said Lambert, "Micky," and Battersby rushed to his assistance, for he knew that he was the one that was needed. Binty Jones had been thrown to the floor by the explosion. As he picked himself up he knew that *Door* had been mortally hit. Then there was another great flash—bigger than any flak shell—a great white soundless explosion right under *Door*'s belly.

"Take a look, Binty," said Lambert. "Back there."

Binty got to his feet while Battersby put his foot on the pilot's seat supports and pressed against the column as hard as he could. His face was beet red and the veins on his forehead shiny with exertion.

The controls remained unyielding, although, with little Battersby there to push, Lambert was able to hold them still. Lambert checked the other controls: the rudder bar was slopping from side to side and the trimmer wheels did not respond. The elevators were unmovable and all the time the aircraft's nose was trying to come up. Both of them were using a lot of energy and Lambert doubted whether they could fight the column forward for the whole trip across the North Sea.

Binty pushed the navigator's curtain aside and was met by a blinding green light. It was so unnatural that he crossed himself and wondered if they had entered Hell as a crew. The green light flickered and died. Suddenly it was pitch dark and there was a stench of burning cordite and rags. Binty Jones edged aft through the darkness. He groped toward Kosher's seat but he was not there. He continued climbing up over the main spar and past the bunk. The interior of the plane was billowing with smoke. Cautiously he stepped into it and walked as far as his turret before he saw the hole in the fuselage. He knew that the metal skin was thin and that a blow with a pencil's end could drive a hole right through it, but that did not lessen the shock of seeing a gap big enough to drive a small car through.

Because the explosion had broken a section of metal skin away from its rivets and bent it back upon itself, the hole was rectangular. The metal rattled angrily in the airstream like a monstrous letterbox flap. For a moment there was less smoke and Binty saw through the hole. There were tripods of gray searchlight beams somewhere near Rotterdam to the east of them, but the Lancaster was turning and the searchlights passed and the smoke closed in again.

"Jesus!" said Binty. He expected a reply from Jimmy Grimm in the turret but when he looked up he found that only the upper half of Jimmy remained. The leather-jacketed torso and masked head was staring over the gun sights as though ready to open fire, but the lower part of him was not there. There was just a boggy puddle of bone splinters, blood and liquidized viscera dumped on the floor and dripping from the flare stowage. Into it was pumping oil from the fractured pipes that led to the rear turret. Binty flashed his torch away from the obscene sight and steadied himself against the ice-cold metal skin of the fuselage.

Lambert had no rudder to steer with.

Experimentally he held the control column and gently turned it sideways to operate the ailerons without letting it back an inch. For what seemed a long time *Door* didn't respond. The fabric covering on the starboard aileron was so tattered that most of the slipstream was whistling through the holes. The port aileron was spoiling the lift on that wing but the starboard one was not giving extra lift to starboard. *Door* settled down like a fitfully sleeping dog and dropped fifty feet with a cranium-pressing lurch that pinned everyone to the floor. When she staggered across the sky Lambert feared the tail had broken but slowly the starboard wing came up. Inch by inch it came until it pointed the way to England. Lambert knew that they had suffered severe structural damage at the rear. He wondered how much warning they would get if the airstream got busy and tried to rip the back end off. Already the drag was such that he could feel the rear part of the aircraft sagging and bucketing. He reduced speed, throttling back to minimize the strain upon the airframe.

Binty plugged into the intercom. "Are you there, Flash?"

There was no reply. "It's Binty, boy. Are you there, kiddo?"

Binty moved gingerly nearer to the gaping holes. Through them he could even see a ragged moon glinting on the black ocean. The floor creaked and tilted under him and nervously he stepped back. There were only a dozen stringers, an ammunition runway and that piece of metal floor plate holding *Creaking Door*'s tail on. Binty's weight might be the last straw.

"Binty, what's happening there?"

"Jimmy's had it, Skip, and I can't get no answer from Flash."

"Can't you open his turret doors?"

"Can't get as far as that, Skip. She's full of smoke. There's half the bloody fuselage side gone. Her tail's hanging on by its teeth."

"Kosher?"

For the first time Binty thought of Kosher. He seemed to have disappeared. "Kosher, you all right?" said Lambert over the intercom. There was an answering noise.

"Where are you?" said Lambert. The intercom gave only a monosyllabic grunt. "You hurt?" Again a bubbling sound came over the wires. Mother, perhaps. They never said Father. Mutti? Yes, it could be Mutti.

Lambert had carried dead and injured before. In 1941 he'd brought a Whitley two hundred and fifty miles with everyone, except himself, dead or semiconscious. By now he knew the signs. The silent ones were either dead or unharmed. The screamers were slightly injured and scared, for no one who was mortally torn could spare the stamina for a long loud scream. It was the soft groans that needed the tourniquets and morphine. Voices like Cohen's.

"Find Kosher, Bint."

"I've found him, Skip."

"Is he O.K.?"

"No." A silence. "You'll have to lose altitude, Skip. He needs oxygen."

"Connect his tube."

"Tube's O.K. He's got no oxygen mask on."

"Put it on."

"Can't, Skip. It's gone."

"What do you mean, gone?"

"Burned away, Skipper. I'm going to have to get the morphine from the box."

Binty went to the rear. This time he stepped lightly and leaned well toward the least damaged side. He tried not to look down into the clouds and sea below and tried to lose weight by willpower.

"How much of this tube of morphine do I put into him?"

"Give him half a tube into the arm. That's still a double dose."

"It's difficult, Skip. I can't tell which is arm. Will the leg be O.K.?" ✴

GO FOR BROKE

from *Journey to Washington*

DANIEL K. INOUYE

When war was first declared, Japanese Americans—even honorably discharged veterans—were
prevented from serving in the armed forces. Then, in the middle of 1942, the 100th Infantry
Battalion was formed from Japanese Americans living in Hawaii. Later, the majority of the men in
the 442nd Regimental Combat Team were from Hawaii. Many of its members had been previously
relocated to internment camps by the government, and still had relatives there.
After being sent to Europe, the regiment was said to have received more commendations than any
other unit in the war, and a nickname: the "Go for Broke Regiment."
Their most famous exploit was the attempted rescue of a Texas National Guard battalion—later
referred to as the Lost Battalion—trapped at the top of a hill surrounded by Germans. The Japanese-
American soldiers rescued 211 of the Texans. They suffered more than 800 casualties in the process.
Senator Daniel K. Inouye of Hawaii served in the 442nd. When he first tried to enlist, he was
rejected because he was training to be a doctor, so he quit his studies.

[ON APRIL 21, 1944] we reached the western edges of the rise where the main line of resistance was anchored long before the frontal assault force. And we didn't mean to sit there and wait for them. We were right under the German guns, 40 yards from their bunkers and rocky defense positions, so close I had to call off our artillery. We had a choice of either moving up or getting the hell out of there.

We moved, hunching slowly up that slope that was so painfully devoid of cover, and almost at once three machine guns opened up on us. I can still smell that piece of unyielding ground under my face, and hear the w-hisss of the bullets tearing the air above my helmet. I lay there for a second,

thinking about how neatly they had pinned us here and wondering how long it would take them to get us all if we just lay there hugging the earth. Then I pulled a grenade from my belt and got up. Sombody punched me in the side, although there wasn't a soul near me, and I sort of fell backward. Then I counted off three seconds as I ran toward that angry splutter of flame at the mouth of the nearest machine gun. I threw the grenade and it cleared the log bunker and exploded in a shower of dust and dirt and metal, and when the gun crew staggered erect I cut them down with my tommy gun. I heard my men pounding up the hill behind me and I waved them toward the left where the other two nests were adjusting their field of fire to cover the whole slope.

"My God, Dan," someone yelled in my ear, "you're bleeding! Get down and I'll get an aid man!"

OPPOSITE:
Dawn Patrol Looks for Enemy
by Rudolph Von Ripper, 1947.

I looked down to where my right hand was clutching my stomach. Blood oozed wet between the fingers. I thought: *That was no punch, you dummy. You took a slug in the gut.*

I wanted to move on; we were pinned down now and the moment was crucial. Unless we stirred, unless we did something quickly, they'd pick us off one at a time. And I knew it was up to me. I lurched up the hill. I lobbed two grenades into the second emplacement before the riflemen guarding it ever saw me. But I had fallen to my knees. Somehow they wouldn't lock and I couldn't stand and I had to pull myself forward with one hand. Someone was hollering, "Come on, you guys, go for broke!" And hunched over, they charged up into the full fire of the third machine gun. And I was so fiercely proud of those guys I wanted to cry.

Then they had to drop and seek protection from the deadly stutter of that last gun. Some of them tried to crawl closer but hadn't a prayer. And all the time I was shuffling my painful way up on the flank of the emplacement, and at last I was close enough to pull the pin on my last grenade. And as I drew my arm back, all in a flash of light and dark I saw him, that faceless German, like a strip of motion picture film running through a projector that's gone berserk. One instant he was standing waist-high in the bunker, and the next he was aiming a rifle grenade at my face from a range of ten yards. And even as I cocked my arm to throw, he fired and his rifle grenade smashed into my right elbow and exploded and all but tore my arm off. I looked at it, stunned and unbelieving. It dangled there by a few bloody shreds of tissue, my grenade still clenched in a fist that suddenly didn't belong to me any more.

It was that grenade that burst into my consciousness, dispelling the unreality of that motion picture in my brain, and the shock of that astounding and spectral moment in time. The grenade mechanism was ticking off the seconds. In two, three or four, it would go off, finishing me and the good men who were rushing up to help me.

"Get back!" I screamed, and swung around to pry the grenade out of that dead fist with my left hand. Then I had it free and I turned to throw and the German was reloading his rifle. But this time I beat him. My grenade blew up in his face and I stumbled to my feet, closing on the bunker, firing my tommy gun left-handed, the useless right arm slapping red and wet against my side. . . .

At the battalion aid station, they fished as much dirt and shrapnel as they could out of my arm and just whistled when they saw the body wound: the bullet had gone in near the right side and come out a slug's width from my spine. Then they put a "Morphine" tag on me, gave me another shot and trundled me into an ambulance for the trip to the field hospital.

I suppose I drifted in and out of coma. Some things stand crystal clear in my mind: somebody yelling to a medic as they were easing me out of the ambulance, "Hold that arm of his, soldier, or it'll fall off of its own weight!"; and a weary-eyed chaplain leaning over me and asking if there was anything I wanted to confess. But hours and whole days are lost in some dark void where I drifted with parched lips and a constant feeling of nausea and wildly-colored dreams of exploding grenades. I remember that first hospital, a tent big enough to house a circus, and all filled with men badly mangled in the machinery of war, all lying under glaring lights and waiting for the team of surgeons who went from table to table snipping and stitching and hadn't even the time to mutter, "Too bad," when they got to a man who was beyond help.

Then they were looming over me, sweaty

A Good Nazi by Alexander P. Russo, 1944.

foreheads and sad eyes peering out above the gauze masks. "Your people were too generous with the morphine, Lieutenant," someone was saying to me. "You might not wake up if we give you any more. You'll have to take this on guts."

I tried to shrug, but by the time I got the message to my good shoulder they'd already started and weren't paying any attention to me. And so I watched the beginning of that operation, the first of eight, and tried not to make any noise when they sliced away the ragged flesh, and wanted to ask them why they didn't just cut the whole damned thing off and be done with it. . . .

Someone came around and showed me a bottle of blood. It had a name on it—Thomas Jefferson Smith, 92nd Division—and while they were rigging it for transfusion into my left arm, I thought how funny that was, showing me the blood, like a waiter display-ing the label on a bottle of wine for your approval. And because I was to have 17 transfusions that first week, half of them

whole blood, I had plenty of opportunity to find out that it wasn't funny at all. A lot of that blood was collected from the 92nd Division itself, and it was shown to the recipient, without comment, as silent evi-dence that fighting men did more than fight, that they cared enough about each other and the men assigned to their sector to donate their blood against that time when somebody, maybe the guy in the next foxhole, would need it to sustain life. And as I thought about the all-Negro 92nd Division and looked at those names— Washington, Woodrow Wilson Peterson—it dawned on me that I was being pumped full of Negro blood. I am very, very grateful for it, and wish I could personally thank every man who donated it for me. . . .

In a few days, I suppose when they became reasonably convinced that I wasn't going to die after all, I was transferred back to the general hospital at Leghorn. And it was there, on May 1, Lei Day in Hawaii, that the gangrene was sufficiently checked so that

104

they could amputate my right arm. It wasn't an emotionally big deal for me. I knew it was coming off and, in fact, had stopped thinking of it as belonging to me for some time. But acceptance and rehabilitation are entirely different things. I had adjusted to the shock *before* the operation. My rehabilitation began almost immediately afterward.

I was staring at the ceiling in the afternoon of my first day as an amputee when a nurse came by and asked if I needed anything. "A cigarette would go pretty good," I said.

"Yes, surely." She smiled and walked off, returning in a few minutes with a fresh pack of Camels. "Here you are, Lieutenant," she said, still smiling, and neatly placed the whole pack on my chest and went on her merry way.

For a while I just stared at it. Then I fingered it with my left hand, trying to decide how I'd go about it if I *did* decide to have a fling at opening it with one hand. I mean, have *you* ever tried opening a pack of cigarettes with one hand?

I sneaked a look around the ward to see if there was anyone in shape to help me, but everyone seemed to be at least as badly off as I was: this was obviously *not* the ward reserved for officers afflicted with athlete's foot and charley horses. Then I began pawing at that cursed pack, holding it under my chin

Battleground before Ortona by Captain Lawrence P. Harris, 1944. Canadian War Museum, Ottawa.

and trying to rip it open with my fingernails. It kept slipping away from me and I kept trying again, sweating in my fury and frustration as freely as if I'd been on a forced march. In fifteen minutes, I'd torn the pack and half the cigarettes in it to shreds, but I'd finally gotten one between my lips. Which is when I realized that that bitch of a nurse hadn't brought me any matches.

I rang the bell and she came sashaying in, still smiling, still trailing that aura of good cheer that made me want to clout her one. "I need a light," I said.

"Oh," she said prettily. "Of course you do." She pulled a pack of matches out of her pocket—she had had them all the time, the dumb broad!—and carefully put them in my hand. And she strolled off again!

If I had obeyed my first instinct I'd have bellowed after her with rage. If I'd obeyed my second instinct, I'd have burst out crying. But let's face it, I was a big boy now, an officer, and I just couldn't let some female Sadsack get the best of me. I just couldn't.

So I started fooling around with the matches. I clutched them and pulled them and twisted them and dropped them, and I never came remotely close to tearing one free, let alone getting it lit. But by this time I had decided that I'd sooner boil in oil before asking *her* for anything again. So I just lay there, fuming silently, and having extremely un-Christian thoughts about that angel of mercy, Miss Whatever-the-hell-her-name-was.

I was on the verge of dozing off when she came around again, *still smiling*. "What's the matter, Lieutenant?" she purred. "Have you decided to quit smoking? It's just as well . . . cigarettes make you cough and . . ."

"I couldn't get the damned thing lit."

She tsk-tsked at her thoughtlessness and sat gracefully on the edge of my bed. "I should have realized," she said, taking the mangled matches from me. "Some amputees like to figure it out for themselves. It gives them a feeling of—well, accomplishment. You know. But it doesn't matter. There'll be lots of things you'll be learning for yourself. We only give you the start."

I just gaped at her. I didn't even know what she was talking about. A start on what? Who needed her? "Look," I growled, "just light the cigarette, will you? I've been three hours trying to get this thing smoked."

"Yes, I know." Nothing ruffled her. Absolutely nothing. "But you see, I won't be around to light your cigarette all the time. You can't depend on other people. Now you have only one hand with which to do all the things that you used to do with two hands. And you have to learn how. We'll start with the matches, all right?"

And damned if she didn't open the cover, bend a match forward, close the cover, flick the match down and light it—all with one hand, all in a split second.

"See?" she said.

"Yes," I whispered.

"Now let's see you do it."

I did it. I lit the cigarette. And all at once her smile wasn't objectionable at all. It was lovely. I wish I could remember her name—I'll never forget her face—but all I remember is that she came from Eagle Pass, Texas, and as far as I was concerned she was the best damn nurse in the United States Army. ✶

From

THE YOUNG LIONS

IRWIN SHAW

In this scene from Shaw's novel, the Allied invasion of France—D Day—is about to begin. Though the specifics of the invasion were secret, even the general public had known for years that it was part of the Allies' strategy. More than 125,000 men were to land on beaches that first day, below cliffs that the German army had spent years fortifying with thick concrete and machine guns. (Many of those bunkers are still in place, too difficult to remove even today.) The Allied troops had been waiting in Britain for months— an excruciating length of time to contemplate the inevitable.

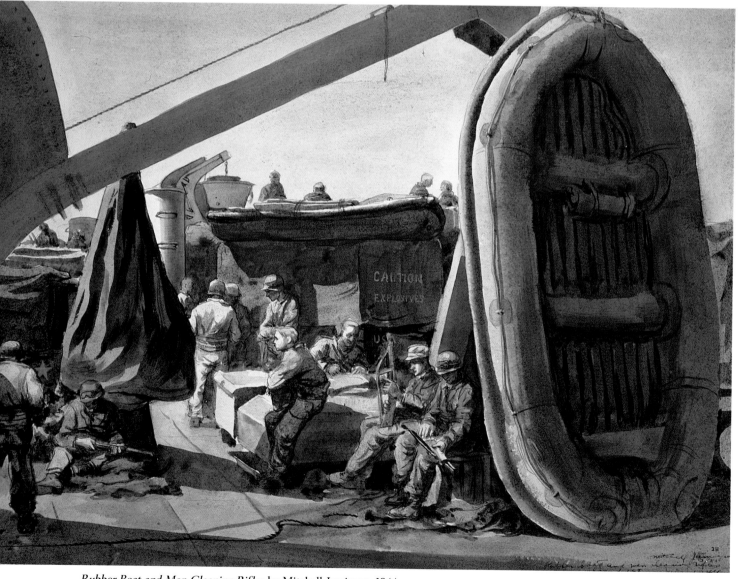

Rubber Boat and Men Cleaning Rifles by Mitchell Jamieson, 1944.

FEAR CAME IN WAVES, during which he could only crouch against the rail, helpless, holding his lips still, not thinking about anything. Then there were periods when he would feel above it all, as though it were not happening to him, as though this could never happen to him, and because it could not happen he could not be hurt, and if he could not be hurt there was nothing to be afraid of. Once he took out his wallet and gravely stared for a long time at the picture of Hope, smiling, holding a fat baby in her arms, the baby with its mouth wide open, yawning.

In the periods when he was not afraid, his mind seemed to run on without conscious direction from him, as though that part of him were bored with the day's activities and was amusing itself in recollections, like a schoolboy dreaming at his desk on a June day with the sun outside the window and the insects humming sleepily over the desks . . . Captain Colclough's speech in the staging area near Southampton a week before (was it only a week, in the sweet-smelling May woods, with the three good meals a day and the barrel of beer in the recreation tent, and the blossoms hanging over the tanks and cannon and the movies twice a day, *Madame Curie*, Greer Garson in a lady-like, well-dressed search for radium, Betty Grable's bare legs—doing God knows what for the morale of the infantry—flickering on the screen that flapped with each gust of wind in the tent, could it only be a week?) . . . "This is the showdown, Men . . ." (Captain Colclough used the word, "Men," twenty times in the speech.) "You're as well trained as any soldiers in the world. When you go onto that beach you're going to be better equipped, better trained, better prepared than the slimy bastards you're going to meet. Every advantage is going to be on your side. Now it is going to be a question of your guts against his. Men, you are going to go in there

and kill the Kraut. That's all you're going to think about from this minute on, killing the bastards. Some of you are going to get hurt, Men, some of you are going to get killed. I'm not going to play it down or make it soft. Maybe a lot of you are going to get killed. . ." He spoke slowly, with satisfaction. "That's what you're in the Army for, Men, that's why you're here, that's why you're going to be put on the beach. If you're not used to that idea yet, get used to it now. I'm not going to dress it up in patriotic speeches. Some of you are going to get killed, but you're going to kill a lot of Germans. If any man . . ." And here he found Noah and stared coldly at him, "If any man here thinks he is going to hold back, or shirk his duty in any way just to save his hide, let him remember that I am going to be along and I am going to see that everyone is going to do his share. This Company is going to be the best damned Company in the Division. I have made up my mind to it, Men. When this battle is over I expect to be promoted to Major. And you men are going to get that promotion for me. I've worked for you and now you are going to work for me. I have an idea the fat-asses in Special Service and Morale back in Washington wouldn't like this speech. I say, screw them. They've had their chance at you, and I haven't interfered. They've filled you full of those goddamn pamphlets and noble sentiments and ping-pong balls, and I've just laid back and let them have their fun. I've let 'em baby you and give you soft titty to suck and put talcum powder on your backsides and make you believe you're all going to live forever and the Army will take care of you like a mother. Now, they're finished, and you don't listen to anyone but me. And here's the gospel for you from now on, straight out of the shit-house—This Company is going to kill more Krauts than any other Company in the Division and I'm going to make Major by

The Battle for Fox Green Beach by Dwight Shepler, 1944.

July fourth, and if that means we're going to have more casualties than anybody else, all I can say is: See the Chaplain, Boys, you didn't come to Europe to tour the monuments. Sergeant, dismiss the Company."

"AttenSHUN! Company, disMISS!"

Captain Colclough had not been seen all day. Perhaps he was below decks preparing another speech to signalize their arrival in France, perhaps he was dead. And Lieutenant Green, who had never made a speech in his life, was pouring sulfanilamide into wounds and covering the dead and grinning at the living and reminding them to keep the barrels of their rifles covered against the water that was spraying over the sides . . .

in for the night among the charred wrecks of barges and bulldozers and splintered fieldpieces. The sound of small-arms fire was quite distant by now, on the other side of the bluff that overlooked the beach. Occasionally a mine went off, and occasionally a shell struck the sand, but it was clear that, for the time being, the beach was secured.

Captain Colclough appeared on deck as the Landing Craft nosed into the shallow water. He had a pearl-handled forty-five in the fancy leather holster at his side. It was a gift from his wife, he had once told somebody in the Company, and he wore it dashingly, low on his thigh, like a sheriff on the cover of a Western magazine.

An Amphibious Engineer Corporal was waving the craft onto the crowded beach. He looked weary, but at ease, as though he had spent most of his life on the coast of France under shell and machine-gun fire.

The ramp went down on the side of the Landing Craft, and Colclough started to lead his Company ashore. Only one of the ramps worked. The other had been torn away when the boat was hit.

Colclough went to the end of the ramp. It led down into the soft sand, and when the waves came in it was under almost three feet of water. Colclough stopped, one foot in the air. Then he pushed back onto the ramp.

"This way, Captain," called the Engineer Corporal.

"There's a mine down there," Colclough said. "Get those men . . ." He pointed to the rest of the squad of Engineers, who were working with a bulldozer, making a road up across the dunes, ". . . to come over here and sweep this area."

"There's no mine there, Captain," said the Corporal wearily.

"I said I saw a mine, Corporal," Colclough shouted.

The Naval Lieutenant who was in command of the vessel pushed his way down the

At four-thirty in the afternoon, the Navy finally got the engines working as Lieutenant Green had promised, and fifteen minutes later, the Landing Craft Infantry slid onto the beach. The beach looked busy and safe, with hundreds of men rushing back and forth, carrying ammunition boxes, piling rations, rolling wire, bringing back wounded, digging

ramp. "Captain," he said anxiously, "will you please get your men off this vessel? I've got to get away from here. I don't want to spend the night on this beach, and my engines aren't strong enough to pull a sick whore off a pisspot. We'll never get off if we hang around another ten minutes."

"There's a mine at the end of the ramp," Colclough said loudly.

"Captain," said the Engineer, "three Companies have come off barges right in this spot and nobody got blown up."

"I gave you a direct order," Colclough said. "Go over and get those men to come here and sweep this area."

"Yes, Sir," said the Engineer, shrugging. He went toward the bulldozer, past a row of sixteen corpses, laid out neatly, in blankets.

"If you don't get off this boat right away," the Naval Lieutenant said, "the United States Navy is going to lose one Landing Craft Infantry."

"Lieutenant," Colclough said coldly, "you pay attention to your business, and I'll pay attention to mine."

"If you're not off in ten minutes," the Lieutenant said, retreating up the ramp, "I am going to take you and your whole god-damned Company out to sea. You'll have to join the Marines to see dry land again."

"This entire matter," said Colclough, "will be reported through proper channels, Lieutenant."

"Ten minutes," the Lieutenant shouted violently over his shoulder, making his way back to his shattered bridge.

"Captain," Lieutenant Green said, in his high voice, from halfway up the crowded ramp, where the men were lined up, peering doubtfully into the dirty green water, on which abandoned Mae Wests, wooden machine-gun ammunition boxes and cardboard K ration cartons were floating soddenly, "Captain," said Lieutenant Green, "I'll be glad to go ahead. As long as the

Corporal said it was all right. Then the men can follow in my footsteps and . . ."

"I am not going to lose any of my men on this beach," Colclough said. "Stay where you are." He gave a slight, decisive hitch to the pearl-handled revolver that his wife had given him. The holster, Noah observed, had a little rawhide fringe on the bottom of it, like the holsters that come with cowboy suits little boys get at Christmas.

The Engineer Corporal was coming back across the beach now, with his Lieutenant. The Lieutenant was a tall, enormous man without a helmet. He was not carrying any weapons. With his windburned, red, sweating face and his huge, dirt-blackened hands hanging out of the sleeves of his rolled-back fatigues, he didn't look like a soldier, but like a foreman on a road gang back home.

"Come on, Captain," the Engineer Lieutenant said. "Come on ashore."

"There's a mine in here," Colclough said. "Get your men over here and sweep the area."

"There's no mine," said the Lieutenant.

"I say I saw a mine."

The men behind the Captain listened uneasily. Now that they were so close to the beach it was intolerable to remain on the craft on which they had suffered so much that day, and which still made a tempting target as it creaked and groaned with the swish of the rollers coming in off the sea. The beach, with its dunes and foxholes and piles of material, looked secure, institutional, homelike, as nothing that floated and was ruled by the Navy could look. They stood behind Colclough, staring at his back, hating him.

The Engineer Lieutenant started to open his mouth to say something to Colclough. Then he looked down and saw the pearl-handled revolver at the Captain's belt. He closed his mouth smiling a little. Then, expressionlessly, without a word, he walked into the water, with his shoes and

One of the Many, #18 by Alexander P. Russo, 1944.

leggings still on, and stamped heavily back and forth, up to the ramp and around it, not paying any attention to the waves that smashed at his thighs. He covered every inch of beach that might possibly have been crossed by any of the men, stamping expressionlessly up and down. Then, without saying another word to Colclough, he stamped back out of the water, his broad back bowed over a little from weariness, and walked heavily back to where his men were running the bulldozer over a huge chunk of concrete with an iron rail sticking out of it.

Colclough wheeled suddenly from his position at the bottom of the ramp, but none of the men was smiling. Then Colclough turned and stepped onto the soil of France, delicately, but with dignity, and one by one his Company followed him, through the cold sea water and the floating debris of the first day of the great battle for the continent of Europe. ✶

Peter McIntyre.

THE LION ROARS

WINSTON CHURCHILL

_____

In September 1938, Britain's prime minister Neville
Chamberlain returned from the Munich Conference
claiming to have tamed Hitler. He said to the nation,
"My good friends, for the second time in our history
a British Prime Minister has returned from
Germany bringing peace with honor. I believe it is
peace for our time. . . . Get a nice quiet sleep."
On May 10, 1940–the day Germany invaded Belgium,
Luxembourg, and the Netherlands–Chamberlain resigned.
The choice of Winston Churchill to lead a coalition
government surprised many. Churchill had been out of
favor for years, banished to the political wilderness. But
the reason for that treatment had been his vocal opposition
to Germany, so he was suddenly in favor again.
Churchill's selection proved essential. He combined
political savvy, military ability, and, of course, an
inspirational eloquence.

"I HAVE NOTHING TO OFFER but blood, toil,
tears and sweat."

> *–May 13, 1940, in his first speech to the*
> *House of Commons as Prime Minister*

"WE SHALL FIGHT on the seas and oceans. We
shall fight with growing confidence and
growing strength in the air. We shall defend
our island, whatever the cost may be. We
shall fight on the beaches. We shall fight on
the landing grounds. We shall fight in the
fields, and in the streets, we shall fight in the
hills. We shall never surrender!"

> *–June 4, 1940, following the Dunkirk*
> *evacuation*

"LET US THEREFORE BRACE OURSELVES to our
duties, and so bear ourselves that if the
British Empire and Commonwealth last for a
thousand years, men will still say, This was
their finest hour."

> *–June 18, 1940, after France fell, leav-*
> *ing Britain the last major European*
> *power opposing Germany*

"NEVER IN THE FIELD OF HUMAN CONFLICT
was so much owed by so many to so few."

> *–August 20, 1940, referring to airmen*
> *fighting the Battle of Britain*

"NEVER GIVE IN—never, never, never, never, in
nothing great or small, large or petty, never
give in except to convictions of honor and
good sense. Never yield to force; never yield
to the apparently overwhelming might of
the enemy."

> *–October 29, 1941 to students at*
> *Harrow school*

"IT WAS THE NATION and the race dwelling all
round the globe that had the lion's heart. I had
the luck to be called upon to give the roar."

> *–November 30, 1954, addressing*
> *Parliament on his 80th birthday*

IV. INHUMANITY

INHUMANITY WAS THE NECESSARY END RESULT of the process that prepared men for war. It made matters quite clear to some: Kill or be killed. It left others confused and uneasy: Were they any better than their enemy?

The British poet Herbert Read, who served in the First World War, made this comment in "To a Conscript of 1940":

> . . . if you can go
> Knowing that there is no reward, no certain use
> In all your sacrifice, then honour is reprieved.
>
> To fight without hope is to fight with grace
> The self reconstructed, the false heart repaired.

Many people, like the author Primo Levi, who writes here of his experience in the Auschwitz concentration camp, were merely victims of the inhumanity. Others laughed it off, seeing it as just more proof of life's essential absurdity. Japanese prison camps were brutal, yet novelist James Clavell, who based *King Rat* on his internment in one, saw something comic among the baser instincts revealed by the experience. But most, especially those directly involved in the war, simply accepted the inhumanity as a fact. When approving novelist Romain Gary's return to combat, General Charles de Gaulle added a reminder: "And don't forget to get killed."

As usual, the individual was subordinated to the machine. But in this war, as D-Day observer Andy Rooney and Iwo Jima witness Edgar L. Jones describe in two selections that follow, the difference in the scale was suddenly much greater than

There were wrecks everywhere—wrecks of vehicles everywhere, wrecks of men everywhere.

—CHARLES EARLY, veteran of the battle of Iwo Jima

A Coast Guardsman stands in silent reverence beside the resting place of a comrade in the Philippines, 1944.
Photo by Coast Guard.

ever before. Navy planes allowed ships to fight without being in sight of each other—a first in naval combat. Artillery was aimed by computer. (ENIAC, the first electronic calculator and grandfather of today's computers, was built for this purpose.)

The scale of the horror appears on the tally sheet of war dead. Expert estimates range from 35 million to 60 million. Either number is unimaginable, and the huge gap between them is itself evidence of the appalling chaos. Yet, reading the works of those who experienced the war firsthand, one sees that the moments of individual terror were just as maddening.

A Group of Polish Prisoners by Elk Eber, 1939. (Captured German Art)

The Opaque Had Become Transparent

CZESLAW MILOSZ

*The Nobel Prize–winning poet was 28 when the Germans
invaded Poland in September 1939.*

WHEN THE BLITZKRIEG BEGAN I felt a need to carry out orders of some sort, and thus to relieve myself of responsibility. Unfortunately, it was not easy to find someone to give orders. But very soon I was wearing something like a uniform made up of ill-matching pieces, unable, however, to revel in any more glorious deeds than taking part in the retreat. The shock of disaster followed immediately. Yet for me that September of 1939 was a breakthrough, which must be hard to imagine for anyone who has never lived through a sudden collapse of the whole structure of collective life. In France, the blitzkrieg did not have the same effect.

I could reduce all that happened to me then to a few things. Lying in the field near a highway bombarded by airplanes, I riveted my eyes on a stone and two blades of grass in front of me. Listening to the whistle of a bomb, I suddenly understood the value of matter: that stone and those two blades of grass formed a whole kingdom, an infinity of forms, shades, textures, lights. They were the universe. I had always refused to accept the division into macro-and micro-cosmos; I preferred to contemplate a piece of bark or a bird's wing rather than sunsets or sunrises. But now I saw, into the depths of matter with exceptional intensity.

Something else was the mixture of fury and relief I felt when I realized that nothing was left of the ministries, offices, and Army. I slept a deep sleep in the hay barns along the way. The nonsense was over at last. That long-dreaded fulfillment had freed us from the self-reassuring lies, illusions, subterfuges; the opaque had become transparent; only a village well, the roof of a hut, or a plough were real, not the speeches of statesmen recalled now with ferocious irony. The land was singularly naked, as it can only be for people without a state, torn from the safety of their habits. ✱

OPPOSITE:
Self Portrait with Jewish Identity Card
by Felix Nussbaum, 1943.
Kulturgheschichtliches Museum Osnabrueck.

From

SCHINDLER'S LIST

THOMAS KENEALLY

---

*Businessman Oskar Schindler used his enamel
factory to shelter 1,300 Polish Jews from the Nazis.
Thomas Keneally's fictionalized biography,
Schindler's Ark, was retitled after the release of the
noted motion picture based on it.*

FROM DIVERSE SOURCES—from the police-man Toffel as well as drunken Bosch of *Ostfaser,* the SS textile operation, Oskar Schindler heard rumors that "procedures in the ghetto" (whatever that meant) were growing more intense. The SS were moving into Cracow some tough *Sonderkommando* units from Lublin, where they had already done sterling work in matters of racial purifi-cation. Toffel had suggested that unless Oskar wanted a break in production, he ought to set up some camp beds for his night shift until after the first Sabbath in June.

So Oskar set up dormitories in the offices and upstairs in the munitions section. Some of the night shift were happy to bed down there. Others had wives, children, par-ents waiting back in the ghetto. Besides, they had the *Blauschein,* the holy blue sticker, on their *Kennkartes.*

On June 3, Abraham Bankier, Oskar's office manager, didn't turn up at Lipowa Street. Schindler was still at home, drinking coffee in Straszewskiego Street, when he got a call from one of his secretaries. She'd seen Bankier marched out of the ghetto, not even stopping at Optima, straight to the Prokocim depot. There'd been other Emalia workers in the group too. There'd been Reich, Leser . . . as many as a dozen.

Oskar called for his car to be brought to him from the garage. He drove over the river and down Lwówska toward Prokocim. There he showed his pass to the guards at the gate. The depot yard itself was full of strings of cattle cars, the station crowded with the ghetto's dispensable citizens standing in orderly lines, convinced still—and perhaps they were right—of the value of passive and orderly response. It was the first time Oskar had seen this juxtaposition of humans and cattle cars, and it was a greater shock than hearing of it; it made him pause on the edge of the platform. Then he saw a jeweler he knew. Seen Bankier? he asked. "He's already in one of the cars, Herr Schindler," said the jeweler. "Where are they taking you?" Oskar asked the man. "We're going to a labor camp,

Live Wire by Tibor Jankay, 1947.

they say. Near Lublin. Probably no worse than . . ." The man waved a hand toward distant Cracow.

Schindler took a pack of cigarettes from his pocket, found some 10-zloty bills and handed the pack and the notes to the jeweler, who thanked him. They had made them leave home without anything this time. They said they'd be forwarding the baggage.

Late the previous year, Schindler had seen in the *SS Bulletin of Budget and Construction* an invitation for bids for the construction of some crematoria in a camp southeast of Lublin. Belzec. Schindler considered the jeweler. Sixty-three or-four. A little thin; had probably had pneumonia last winter. Worn pin-striped suit, too warm for the day. And in the clear, knowing eyes a capacity to bear finite suffering. Even in the summer of 1942 it was impossible to guess at the connections between such a man as this and those ovens of extraordinary cubic capacity. Did they intend to start epidemics among the prisoners? Was that to be the method?

Beginning from the engine, Schindler moved along the line of more than twenty cattle cars, calling Bankier's name to the faces peering down at him from the open grillwork high above the slats of the cars. It was fortunate for Abraham that Oskar did not ask himself why it was Bankier's name he called, that he did not pause and consider that Bankier's had only equal value to all the other names loaded aboard the *Ostbahn* rolling stock. An existentialist might have been defeated by the numbers at Prokocim, stunned by the equal appeal of all the names and voices. But Schindler was a philosophic innocent. He knew the people he knew. He knew the name of *Bankier. "Bankier! Bankier!"* he continued to call.

He was intercepted by a young *SS Oberscharführer,* an expert railroad shipper from Lublin. He asked for Schindler's pass. Oskar could see in the man's left hand an enormous list—pages of names.

My workers, said Schindler. Essential industrial workers. My office manager. It's idiocy. I have Armaments Inspectorate contracts, and here you are taking the workers I need to fulfill them.

You can't have them back, said the young man. They're on the list. The SS NCO knew from experience that the list conferred an equal destination on all its members.

Oskar dropped his voice to that hard murmur, the growl of a reasonable man, well-connected, who wasn't going to bring up all his heavy guns yet. Did the *Herr Oberscharführer* know how long it would take to train experts to replace those on the list? At my works, Deutsche Email Fabrik, I have a munitions section under the special

protection of General Schindler, my namesake. Not only would the *Oberscharführer's* comrades on the Russian Front be affected by the disruption of production, but the office of the Armaments Inspectorate would demand explanations as well.

The young man shook his head—just a harassed transit official. "I've heard that kind of story before, sir," he said. But he was worried. Oskar could tell it and kept leaning over him and speaking softly with an edge of menace. "It's not my place to argue with the list," said Oskar. "Where is your superior officer?"

The young man nodded toward an SS officer, a man in his thirties wearing a frown above his spectacles. "May I have your name, *Herr Unstersturmführer?"* Oskar asked him, already pulling a notebook from his suit pocket.

The officer also made a statement about the holiness of the list. For this man it was the secure, rational, and sole basis for all this milling of Jews and movement of rail cars. But Schindler got crisper now. He'd heard about the list, he said. What he had asked was what the *Unstersturmführer's* name was. He intended to appeal directly to *Oberführer* Scherner and to General Schindler of the Armaments Inspectorate.

"Schindler?" asked the officer. For the first time he took a careful look at Oskar. The man was dressed like a tycoon, wore the right badge, had generals in the family. "I believe I can guarantee you, *Herr Unstersturmführer,"* said Schindler in his benign grumble, "that you'll be in southern Russia within the week."

The NCO going ahead, Herr Schindler and the officer marched side by side between the ranks of prisoners and the loaded cattle cars. The locomotive was already steaming and the engineer leaning from his cabin, looking down the length of the train, waiting to be dispatched. The officer called to *Ostbahn* officials they passed on

the platform to hold up. At last they reached one of the rear cars. There were a dozen workers in there with Bankier; they had all boarded together as if expecting a joint deliverance. The door was unlocked and they jumped down—Bankier and Frankel from the office; Reich, Leser, and the others from the factory. They were restrained, not wanting to permit anyone to detect their pleasure at being saved the journey. Those left inside began chattering merrily, as if they were fortunate to be traveling with so much extra room, while with emphasis in his pen strokes, the officer removed the Emalia workers one at a time from the list and required Oskar to initial the pages.

As Schindler thanked the officer and turned to follow his workers away, the man detained him by the elbow of his suit coat. "Sir," he said, "it makes no difference to us, you understand. We don't care whether it's this dozen or that."

The officer, who had been frowning when Oskar first saw him, now seemed calm, as if he had discovered the theorem behind the situation. You think your thirteen little tinsmiths are important? We'll replace them with another thirteen little tinsmiths and all your sentimentality for these will be defeated. "It's the inconvenience to the list, that's all," the officer explained. ✶

Other individuals also sheltered or gave aid to Jews hoping to escape Nazi territory. Chiune Sugihara, a Japanese diplomat in Lithuania, disregarded orders and issued more than 2,000 visas. Raoul Wallenberg, a Swedish diplomat, traveled to Hungary in 1944 to help Jews escape. He is credited with saving anywhere from 4,000 to 35,000 lives.

Study C, by Samuel Bak, 1995.
Courtesy Pucker Gallery, Boston, MA.

From

If This Is a Man

(Survival in Auschwitz)

PRIMO LEVI

Nazi persecution of Jews began almost as soon as Hitler took power in 1933. In early 1942, German bureaucrats held the Wannsee Conference, agreeing upon a "final solution" and an efficient method: Jews would be transported to camps where they could be systematically exterminated. Gypsies, Slavs, and homosexuals were also marked for death or slave labor. In early 1944, author Primo Levi was transferred from an Italian prison camp to Auschwitz.

THE LORRY STOPPED, and we saw a large door, and above it a sign, brightly illuminated (its memory still strikes me in my dreams): *Arbeit Macht Frei*, work gives freedom.

We climb down, they make us enter an enormous empty room that is poorly heated. We have a terrible thirst. The weak gurgle of the water in the radiators makes us ferocious; we have had nothing to drink for four days. But there is also a tap—and above it a card which says that it is forbidden to drink as the water is dirty. Nonsense. It seems obvious that the card is a joke, "they" know that we are dying of thirst and they put us in a room, and there is a tap, and *Wassertrinken Verboten*. I drink and I incite my companions to do likewise, but I have to spit it out, the water is tepid and sweetish, with the smell of a swamp.

This is hell. Today, in our times, hell must be like this. A huge, empty room: we are tired, standing on our feet, with a tap which

drips while we cannot drink the water, and we wait for something which will certainly be terrible, and nothing happens and nothing continues to happen. What can one think about? One cannot think any more, it is like being already dead. Someone sits down on the ground. The time passes drop by drop.

We are not dead. The door is opened and an SS man enters, smoking. He looks at us slowly and asks, *"Wer kann Deutsch?"* One of us whom I have never seen, named Flesch, moves forward; he will be our interpreter. The SS man makes a long calm speech; the interpreter translates. We have to form rows of five, with intervals of two yards between man and man; then we have to undress and make a bundle of the clothes in a special manner, the woollen garments on one side, all the rest on the other, we must take off our shoes but pay great attention that they are not stolen.

Stolen by whom? Why should our shoes be stolen? And what about our documents, the few things we have in our pockets, our watches? We all look at the interpreter, and the interpreter asks the German, and the German smokes and looks him through and through as if he were transparent, as if no one had spoken.

I had never seen old men naked. Mr. Bergmann wore a truss and asked the interpreter if he should take it off, and the interpreter hesitated. But the German understood and spoke seriously to the interpreter pointing to someone. We saw the interpreter swallow and then he said: "The officer says, take off the truss, and you will be given that of Mr. Coen." One could see the words coming bitterly out of Flesch's mouth; this was the German manner of laughing.

Now another German comes and tells us to put the shoes in a certain corner, and we put them there, because now it is all over and we feel outside this world and the only thing is to obey. Someone comes with a broom and sweeps away all the shoes, outside the door in

1943 AD by Ben Shahn, 1943. © Estate of Ben Shahn/Licensed by VAGA, NY.
Courtesy The Syracuse University Art Collection, NY.

a heap. He is crazy, he is mixing them all together, ninety-six pairs, they will be all unmatched. The outside door opens, a freezing wind enters and we are naked and cover ourselves up with our arms. The wind blows and slams the door; the German reopens it and stands watching with interest how we writhe to hide from the wind, one behind the other. Then he leaves and closes it.

Now the second act begins. Four men with razors, soapbrushes and clippers burst in; they have trousers and jackets with stripes, with a number sewn on the front; perhaps they are the same sort as those others of this evening (this evening or yesterday evening?); but these are robust and flourishing. We ask many questions but they catch hold of us and in a moment we find ourselves shaved and sheared. What comic faces we have without hair! The four speak a language which does not seem of this world. It is certainly not German, for I understand a little German.

Finally another door is opened: here we are, locked in, naked, sheared and standing, with our feet in water—it is a shower-room. We are alone. Slowly the astonishment

126

dissolves, and we speak, and everyone asks questions and no one answers. If we are naked in a shower-room, it means that we will have a shower. If we have a shower it is because they are not going to kill us yet. But why then do they keep us standing, and give us nothing to drink, while nobody explains anything, and we have no shoes or clothes, but we are all naked with our feet in the water, and we have been travelling five days and cannot even sit down.

And our women?

Mr. Levi asks me if I think that our women are like us at this moment, and where they are, and if we will be able to see them again. I say yes, because he is married and has a daughter; certainly we will see them again. But by now my belief is that all this is a game to mock and sneer at us. Clearly they will kill us, whoever thinks he is going to live is mad, it means that he has swallowed the bait, but I have not; I have understood that it will soon all be over, perhaps in this same room, when they get bored

of seeing us naked, dancing from foot to foot and trying every now and again to sit down on the floor. But there are two inches of cold water and we cannot sit down.

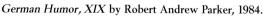

. . . *HÄFTLING* [PRISONER]: I have learnt that I am Häftling. My number is 174517; we have been baptized, we will carry the tattoo on our left arm until we die.

The operation was slightly painful and extraordinarily rapid: they placed us all in a row, and one by one, according to the alphabetical order of our names, we filed past a skilful official, armed with a sort of pointed tool with a very short needle. It seems that this is the real, true initiation: only by "showing one's number" can one get bread and soup. Several days passed, and not a few cuffs and punches, before we became used to showing our number promptly enough not to disorder the daily operation of food-distribution: weeks and months were needed to learn its sound in the German language.

German Humor, XIX by Robert Andrew Parker, 1984.

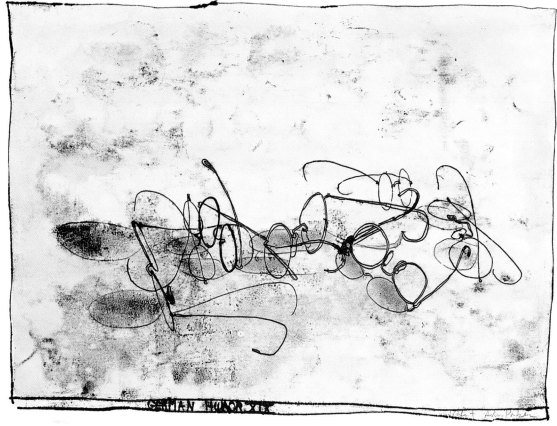

And for many days, while the habits of freedom still led me to look for the time on my wristwatch, my new name ironically appeared instead, a number tattooed in bluish characters under the skin.

Only much later, and slowly, a few of us learnt something of the funereal science of the numbers of Auschwitz, which epitomize the stages of destruction of European Judaism. To the old hands of the camp, the numbers told everything: the period of entry into the camp, the convoy of which one formed a part, and consequently the nationality. Everyone will treat with respect the numbers from 30,000 to 80,000: there are only a few hundred left and they represented the few survivals from the Polish ghettos. It is as well to watch out in commercial dealings with a 116,000 or a 117,000: they now number only about forty, but they represent the Greeks of Salonica, so take care they do not pull the wool over your eyes. As for the high numbers, they carry an essentially comic air about them, like the words "freshman" or "conscript" in ordinary life. The typical high number is a corpulent, docile and stupid fellow: he can be convinced that leather shoes are distributed at the infirmary to all those with delicate feet, and can be persuaded to run there and leave his bowl of soup "in your custody"; you can sell him a spoon for three rations of bread; you can send him to the most ferocious of the Kapos to ask him (as happened to me!) if it is true that his is the *Kartoffelschalenkommando*, the "Potato Peeling Command" and if one can be enrolled in it.

In fact, the whole process of introduction to what was for us a new order took place in a grotesque and sarcastic manner. When the tattooing operation was finished, they shut us in a vacant hut. The bunks are made, but we are severely forbidden to touch or sit on them: so we wander around aimlessly for half the day in the limited space available, still tormented by the parching thirst of the journey. Then the door opens and a boy in a striped suit comes in, with a fairly civilized air, small, thin and blond. He speaks French and we throng around him with a flood of questions which till now we had asked each other in vain.

But he does not speak willingly; no one here speaks willingly. We are new, we have nothing and we know nothing; why waste time on us? He reluctantly explains to us that all the others are out at work and will come back in the evening. He has come out of the infirmary this morning and is exempt from work for today. I asked him (with an ingenuousness that only a few days later already seemed incredible to me) if at least they would give us back our toothbrushes. He did not laugh, but with his face animated by fierce contempt, he threw at me "*Vous n'êtes pas a la maison.*" And it is this refrain that we hear repeated by everyone. You are not at home, this is not a sanatorium, the only exit is by way of the Chimney. (What did it mean? Soon we were all to learn what it meant.)

And it was in fact so. Driven by thirst, I eyed a fine icicle outside the window, within hand's reach. I opened the window and broke off the icicle but at once a large, heavy guard prowling outside brutally snatched it away from me. "*Warum?*" I asked him in my poor German. "*Hier ist kein warum*" (there is no why here), he replied, pushing me inside with a shove.

The explanation is repugnant but simple: in this place everything is forbidden, not for hidden reasons, but because the camp has been created for that purpose. . . . Hour after hour, this first long day of limbo draws to its end. ✱

Estimates of the death toll vary, but it is likely that nearly six million Jews and almost half a million Gypsies were killed before the camps were liberated.

OPPOSITE:
Invasion Craft—Sicily
by Mitchell Jamieson, 1943.

WHAT IS TERRIBLE

ROY FULLER

*Fuller, who went on to become a well–known poet and
novelist, served in the Royal Navy.*

Life at last I know is terrible:
The innocent scene, the innocent walls and light
And hills for me are like the cavities
Of surgery and dreams. The visible might
Vanish, for all it reassures, in white.

This apprehension has come slowly to me,
Like symptoms and bulletins of sickness. I
Must first be moved across two oceans, then
Bored, systematically and sickeningly,
In a place where war is news. And constantly

I must be threatened with what is certainly worse:
Peril and death, but no less boring. And
What else? Besides my fear, my misspent time,
My love, hurt and postponed, there is the hand
Moving the empty glove; the bland

Aspect of nothing disguised as something; that
Part of living incommunicable,
For which we try to find vague adequate
Images, and which, after all,
Is quite surprisingly communicable.

Because in the clear hard light of war the ghosts
Are seen to be suspended by wires, and in
The old house the attic is empty: and the furious
Inner existence of objects and even
Ourselves is largely a myth: and for the sin

To blame our fathers, to attribute vengeance
To the pursuing chorus, and to live
In a good and tenuous world of private values,
Is simply to lie when only truth can give
Continuation in time to bread and love.

For what is terrible is the obvious
Organization of life: the oiled black gun,
And what it cost, the destruction of Europe by
Its councils; the unending justification
Of that which cannot be justified, what is done.

The year, the month, the day, the minute at war
Is terrible and my participation
And that of all the world is terrible.
My living must bear the laceration
Of the herd, and always will. What's done

To me is done to many. I can see
No ghosts, but only the fearful actual
Lives of my comrades. If the empty whitish
Horror is ever to be flushed and real,
It must be for them and changed by them all.

DIGGING IN A FOOTLOCKER

WALTER McDONALD

Crouched before dismantled guns,
we found war souvenirs
our uncle padlocked in the attic,
a brittle latch easily pried off.

Stiff uniforms on top, snapshots
of soldiers young as our cousins,
a velvet box of medals
as if he fought all battles

in World War II. Bayonets, machetes,
a folded flag, two hand grenades
with missing pins. We picked up teeth
like pennies, loose, as if tossed in,

a piece of something dark and waxy
like a fig, curved like a question mark,
a human ear. We touched dried pieces
of cloth stuck to curved bones

and held them up to the light,
turning them over and over, wondering
how did uncles learn to kill,
what would happen when we grew up.

From *Small Wonder: Worlds in a Box* by David Levinthal, 1996.

Night Work by Kerr Eby, 1944.

UNSEEN FIRE

R. N. CURREY

This is a damned inhuman sort of war.
I have been fighting in a dressing-gown
Most of the night; I cannot see the guns,
The sweating gun-detachments or the planes;

I sweat down here before a symbol thrown
Upon a screen, sift facts, initiate
Swift calculations and swift orders; wait
For the precise split-second to order fire.

We chant our ritual words; beyond the phones
A ghost repeats the orders to the guns:
One Fire . . . Two Fire . . . ghosts answer: the guns roar
Abruptly; and an aircraft waging war
Inhumanly from nearly five miles height
Meets our bouquet of death—and turns sharp right.

WE REGRET OUR MISTAKE

ARMY AIR CORPS

EXAMINING BOARD FOR AIR CORPS FLYING CADETS
Maxwell Field, Alabama

31/rb
October 11, 1940

Mr. Garland Fort Pinkston.
Gardova, Tennessee.

Dear Sir:

Through the most unfortunate circumstances, your application was allowed to be completed because of our ignorance of your race. At the present time the United States Army is not training any except members of the White race for duty as pilots of military aircraft. Such training may be begun during this present national emergency and it is suggested that all papers being returned to you herewith, be held in readiness so that in event the above mentioned training becomes an actuality, your application may be reopened.

Please accept our sincerest apologies for allowing you to go to so much trouble through our oversight in connection with your original letter to this Board.

Very truly yours,
HERBERT M. WEST, JR.
1st Lieutenant, Air Corps.
Recorder.

In early 1941, the army gave in to pressure from civil rights groups and formed the 99th Pursuit Squadron, which trained at a segregated airfield in Tuskegee, Alabama. Though politics kept the unit out of combat until the middle of 1943, it distinguished itself for the rest of the war. It was the only fighter escort group that did not lose a bomber.

OPPOSITE:
War Series: Victory by Jacob Lawrence, 1947.
Collection of Whitney Museum of American Art, NY.

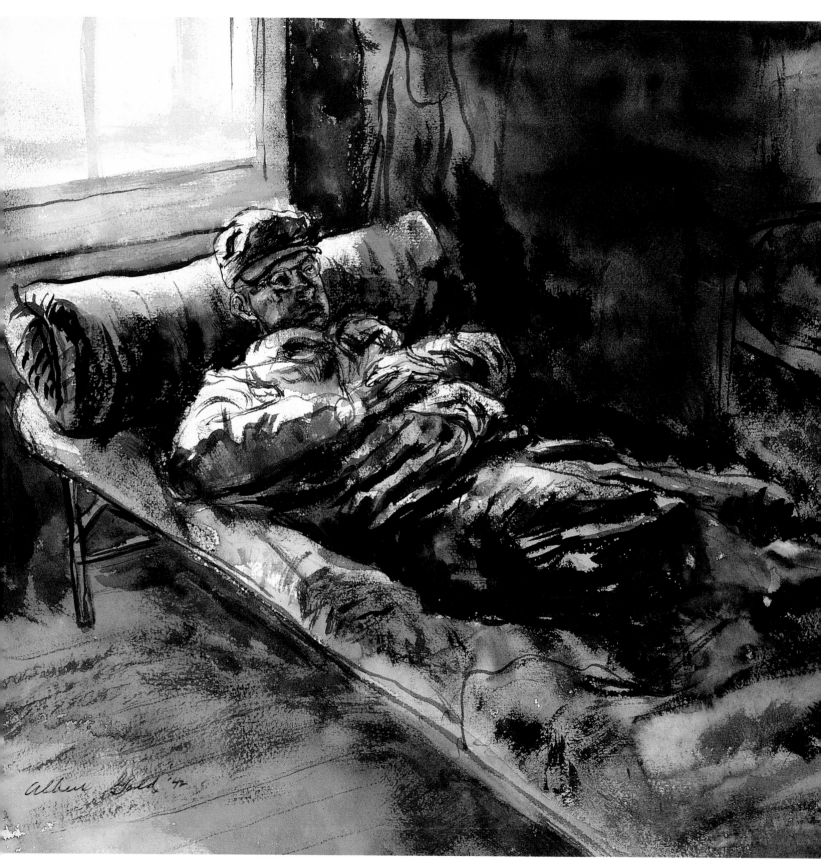

Homesick, Barracks at Fort Belvoir, Virginia by Albert Gold, 1942.
Courtesy D. Wigmore Fine Art, Inc., NY.

From

The Naked and the Dead

NORMAN MAILER

Drafted in 1944 after graduating with an engineering degree from Harvard, Mailer served in the Pacific as a surveyor, intelligence clerk, and rifleman.

NOBODY COULD SLEEP. When morning came, assault craft would be lowered and a first wave of troops would ride through the surf and charge ashore on the beach at Anopopei. All over the ship, all through the convoy, there was a knowledge that in a few hours some of them were going to be dead.

A SOLDIER LIES FLAT ON HIS BUNK, closes his eyes, and remains wideawake. All about him, like the soughing of surf, he hears the murmurs of men dozing fitfully. "I won't do it, I won't do it," someone cries out of a dream, and the soldier opens his eyes and gazes slowly about the hold, his vision becoming lost in the intricate tangle of hammocks and naked bodies and dangling equipment. He decides he wants to go to the head, and cursing a little, he wriggles up to a sitting position, his legs hanging over the bunk, the steel pipe of the hammock above cutting across his hunched back. He sighs, reaches for his shoes, which he has tied to a stanchion, and slowly puts them on. His bunk is the fourth in a tier of five, and he climbs down uncertainly in the half-darkness, afraid of stepping on one of the men in the hammocks below him. On the floor he picks his way through a tangle of bags and packs, way through a tangle of bags and packs, stumbles once over a rifle, and makes his way to the bulkhead door. He passes through another hold whose aisle is just as cluttered, and finally reaches the head.

Inside the air is steaming. Even now a man is using the sole fresh-water shower, which has been occupied ever since the troops have come on board. The soldier walks past the crap games in the unused salt-water shower stalls, and squats down on the wet split boards of the latrine. He has forgotten his cigarettes and he bums one from a man sitting a few feet away. As he smokes he looks at the black wet floor littered with butts, and listens to the water sloshing through the latrine box. There has been really no excuse for coming, but he continues to sit on the box because it is cooler here, and the odor of the latrine, the brine, the chlorine, the clammy bland smell of wet metal is less oppressive than the heavy sweating fetor of the troop holds. The soldier remains for a long time, and then slowly he stands up, hoists his green fatigue pants, and thinks of the struggle to get back to his bunk. He knows he will lie there waiting for the dawn and he says to himself, I wish it was time already, I don't give a damn, I wish it was time already. ✳

FOLLOWING PAGES:
Troop Transport by Albert Gold, 1945.
Courtesy D. Wigmore Fine Art, Inc., NY.

THE DEATH OF THE BALL TURRET GUNNER

RANDALL JARRELL

Jarrell, then aged 28, enlisted in the Army Air Corps in 1942.

From my mother's sleep I fell into the State,
And I hunched in its belly till my wet fur froze.
Six miles from earth, loosed from its dream of life,
I woke to black flak and the nightmare fighters.
When I died they washed me out of the turret with a hose.

Tail Gunner by Flight Lieutenant Paul Goranson, 1943. Canadian War Museum, Ottawa.

Lts. Donovan and Peterson returned from their long stay at the modification center in Evansville, Ind. Perfect flying weather held out from 0700 until after dark. Capt. Douglas, Lts. Liston, Bayle, McLachlan, Moist and Myers opened the night flying season — so, the worst is here — with a six-ship formation ride that lasted until 2230.

SQUADRON	DAY'S TOTAL	MONTH'S TOTAL
320 -	158.3	1203.8
321 -	158.5	1379.9
322 -	121.2	1221.8

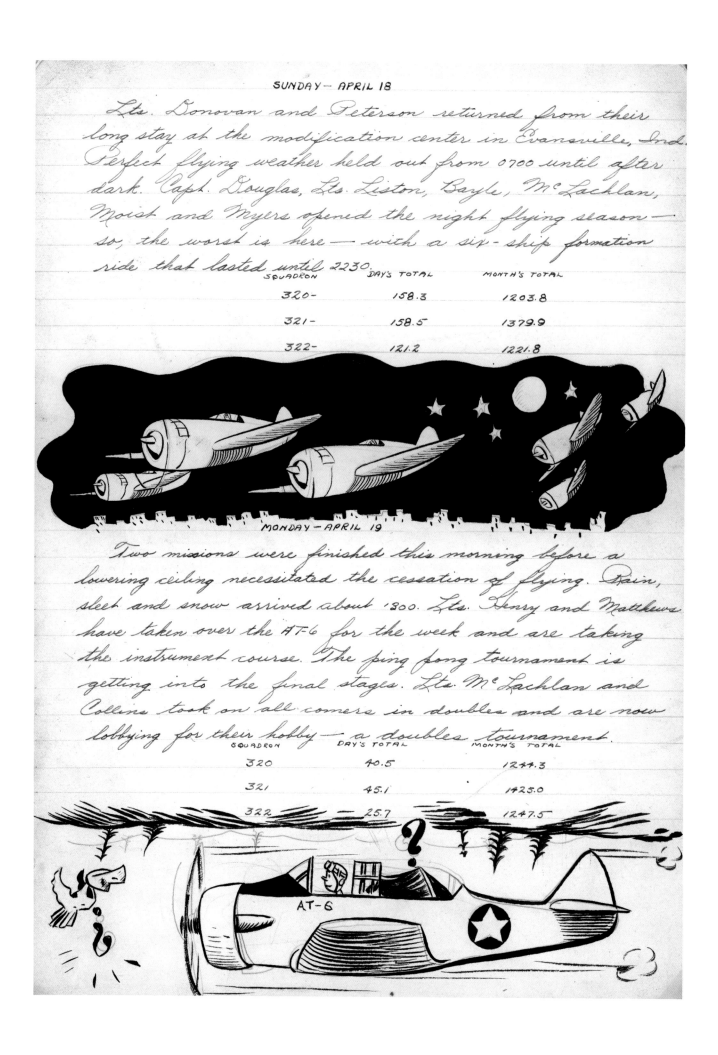

MONDAY — APRIL 19

Two missions were finished this morning before a lowering ceiling necessitated the cessation of flying. Rain, sleet and snow arrived about 1300. Lts. Henry and Matthews have taken over the AT-6 for the week and are taking the instrument course. The ping pong tournament is getting into the final stages. Lts. McLachlan and Collins took on all comers in doubles and are now lobbying for their hobby — a doubles tournament.

SQUADRON	DAY'S TOTAL	MONTH'S TOTAL
320	40.5	1244.3
321	45.1	1425.0
322	25.7	1247.5

From

CATCH-22

JOSEPH HELLER

This novel about insanity made so much sense that its title, connoting an absurd bureaucratic paradox, now appears in the Oxford English Dictionary. *At the story's center is the bombardier Yossarian, who has seen enough war. Though the army isn't yet ready to discharge him, he has a plan that seems foolproof.*

YOSSARIAN ... decided right then and there to go crazy.

"You're wasting your time," Doc Daneeka was forced to tell him.

"Can't you ground someone who's crazy?"

"Oh, sure. I have to. There's a rule saying I have to ground anyone who's crazy."

"Then why don't you ground me? I'm crazy. Ask Clevinger."

"Clevinger? Where *is* Clevinger? You find Clevinger and I'll ask him."

"Then ask any of the others. They'll tell you how crazy I am."

"They're crazy."

"Then why don't you ground them?"

"Why don't they ask me to ground them?"

"Because they're crazy, that's why."

"Of course they're crazy," Doc Daneeka replied. "I just told you they're crazy, didn't I? And you can't let crazy people decide whether you're crazy or not, can you?"

Yossarian looked at him soberly and tried another approach. "Is Orr crazy?"

"He sure is," Doc Daneeka said.

"Can you ground him?"

"I sure can. But first he has to ask me to. That's part of the rule."

"Then why doesn't he ask you to?"

"Because he's crazy," Doc Daneeka said. "He has to be crazy to keep flying combat missions after all the close calls he's had. Sure, I can ground Orr. But first he has to ask me to."

"That's all he has to do to be grounded?"

"That's all. Let him ask me."

"And then you can ground him?" Yossarian asked.

"No. Then I can't ground him."

"You mean there's a catch?"

"Sure there's a catch," Doc Daneeka replied. "Catch-22. Anyone who wants to get out of combat duty isn't really crazy."

There was only one catch and that was Catch-22, which specified that a concern for one's own safety in the face of dangers that were real and immediate was the process of a rational mind. Orr was crazy and could be grounded. All he had to do was ask; and as soon as he did, he would no longer be crazy and would have to fly more missions. Orr would be crazy to fly more missions and sane if he didn't, but if he was sane he had to fly them. If he flew them he was crazy and didn't have to; but if he didn't want to he was sane and had to. Yossarian was moved very deeply by the absolute simplicity of this clause of Catch-22 and let out a respectful whistle.

"That's some catch, that Catch-22," he observed.

"It's the best there is," Doc Daneeka agreed. ✶

D-DAY

On June 6, 1944, D-Day, hundreds of thousands of Allied troops embarked from England in a crucial operation, the invasion of German-occupied France. Novelist Irwin Shaw and Lt. Robert Edlin were both members of the invasion force. Television commentator Andy Rooney saw the operation as a reporter for the army newspaper Stars and Stripes.

From
THE YOUNG LIONS

IRWIN SHAW

A BATTLE EXISTS on many different levels. There is the purely moral level, at the Supreme Headquarters perhaps eighty miles away from the sound of the guns, where the filing cabinets have been dusted in the morning, where there is a sense of quiet and efficiency, where soldiers who never fire a gun and never have a shot fired at them, the high Generals, sit in their pressed uniforms and prepare statements to the effect that all has been done that is humanly possible, the rest being left to the judgment of God, Who has risen early, ostensibly, for this day's work, and is partially and critically regarding the ships, the men drowning in the water, the flight of high explosive, the accuracy of bombardiers, the skill of naval officers, the bodies being thrown into the air by mines, the swirl of tides against steel spikes at the water's edge,

the loading of cannon in gun emplacements, and the building far back from the small violent fringe between the two armies, where the files have also been dusted that morning and the enemy Generals sit in different pressed uniforms, looking at very similar maps, reading very similar reports, matching their moral strength and intellectual ingenuity with their colleagues and antagonists a hundred miles away. In these places, in the rooms where the large maps with the acetate overlays and the red and black crayon markings are hung on the walls, the battle swiftly takes on an orderly and formal appearance. A plan is always in process of being worked out on the maps. If Plan I fails, Plan II is attempted. If Plan II is only partially successful, a pre-arranged modification of Plan III is instituted. The Generals have all studied from the same books at West Point and Spandau and Sandhurst, and many of them have written books themselves and read each other's works, and they all know what Caesar did in a somewhat similar situation and the mistake that Napoleon made in Italy and how Ludendorff failed to exploit a break in the line in 1915, and they all hope, on opposite sides of the English Channel, that the situation never gets to that decisive point where they will have to say the Yes or the No which

R.A.F. Command Center by Robert Andrew Parker, 1981.

may decide the fate of the battle, and perhaps the nation, and which takes the last trembling dram of courage out of a man, and which may leave him ruined and broken for the rest of his life, all his honors gone, his reputation empty, when he has said it. So they sit back in their offices, which are like the offices of General Motors or the offices of I. G. Farben in Frankfurt, with stenographers and typists and flirtations in the halls, and look at the maps and read the reports and pray that Plans I, II, and III will operate as everyone has said they will operate back on Grosvenor Square and the Wilhelmstrasse, with only small, not very important modifications that can be handled locally, by the men on the scene.

The men on the scene see the affair on a different level. They have not been questioned on the proper manner of isolating the battlefield. They have not been consulted on the length of the preliminary bombardment. Meteorologists have not instructed them on

144

the rise and fall of the tides in the month of June or the probable incidence of storms. They have not been at the conferences in which was discussed the number of divisions it would be profitable to lose to reach a phase line one mile inland by 1600 hours. There are no filing cabinets on board the landing barges, no stenographers with whom to flirt, no maps in which their actions, multiplied by two million, become clear, organized, intelligent symbols, suitable for publicity releases and the tables of historians.

They see helmets, vomit, green water, shell geysers, smoke, crashing planes, blood plasma, submerged obstacles, guns, pale, senseless faces, a confused drowning mob of men running and falling, that seem to have no relation to any of the things they have been taught since they left their jobs and wives to put on the uniform of their country. To a General sitting before the maps eighty miles away, with echoes of Caesar and Clausewitz and Napoleon fleetingly swimming through his brain, matters are proceeding as planned, or almost as planned, but to the man on the scene everything is going wrong.

Taking Cover by David Fredenthal, 1943.

"Oh, God," sobs the man on the scene, when the shell hits the Landing Craft Infantry, H hour plus two, one mile out from shore, and the wounded begin to scream on the slippery decks, "Oh, God, it is all screwed up."

To the Generals eighty miles away, the reports on casualties are encouraging. To the man on the scene the casualties are never encouraging. When he is hit or when the man next to him is hit, when the ship fifty feet away explodes, when the Naval Ensign on the bridge is screaming in a high, girlish voice for his mother because he has nothing left below his belt, it can only appear to him that he has been involved in a terrible accident, and it is inconceivable at that moment to believe that there is a man eighty miles away who has foreseen that accident, encouraged it, made arrangements for it to happen, and who can report, after it has happened (although he must know about the shell, about the listing Landing Craft Infantry, about the wet decks and the screaming Ensign) that everything is going according to plan.

"Oh, God," sobs the man on the scene, watching the amphibious tanks sink under the waves, with perhaps one man swimming up out of the hatch, "Oh, God," he sobs, looking down at the queer, unattached leg lying beside his face and realizing it is his, "Oh, God," as the ramp goes down and the twelve men in front of him pile up in the cold two feet of water, with the machine-gun bullets inside them, "Oh, God," looking for the holes on the beach he has been told the Air Force was going to put there for him, and not finding them, and lying there face down, with the mortar shell dropping silently on top of him, "Oh, God," he sobs, seeing the friend he has loved since Fort Benning, Georgia, in 1940, blow up on a mine and hang across a barbed-wire fence with his back wide open from neck to hip, "Oh, God," sobs the man on the scene, "it is all screwed up." ✶

The Drop—Paratroopers by Albert Richards, 1944. Imperial War Museum, London.

From MY WAR

ANDY ROONEY

THERE HAVE BEEN only a handful of days since the beginning of time on which the direction the world was taking has been changed for the better in one twenty-four-hour period by an act of man. June 6, 1944, was one of them. What the Americans, the British, and the Canadians were trying to do was get back a whole continent that had been taken from its rightful owners and whose cit-izens had been taken captive by Adolf Hitler's German army. It was one of the most monumentally unselfish things one group of people ever did for another.

. . . If you're young, and not really clear what D-Day was, let me tell you, it was a day unlike any other. I landed on Utah Beach several days after the first assault waves went in on the morning of June 6. I am uncertain of the day. When I came in, row on row of dead American soldiers were laid out on the sand just above the high-tide mark where the beach turned into weedy clumps of grass. They were covered with olive-drab blankets, just their feet sticking out at the bottom, their GI boots sticking out. I remember their boots—all the same on

Compassion by Howard Brodie, 1945.

such different boys. They had been dead several days and some of them had been killed, not on the beaches, but inland.

No one can tell the whole story of D-Day because no one knows it. Each of the 60,000 men who waded ashore that day knew a little part of the story too well. To them, the landing looked like a catastrophe. Each knew a friend shot through the throat, shot through the knee. Each knew the names of five hanging dead on the barbed wire in the water twenty yards offshore, three who lay unattended on the stony beach as the blood drained from holes in their bodies. They saw whole tank crews drowned when the tanks rumbled off the ramps of their landing craft and dropped into twenty feet of water.

. . . Across the Channel in Allied head-quarters in England, the war directors, remote from the details of tragedy, were exultant. They saw no blood, no dead, no dying. From the statisticians' point of view, the invasion was a great success. The statisticians were right. They always are—that's the damned thing about it. ★

From Gerald Astor's

VOICES OF D-DAY

LT. ROBERT EDLIN

IT SEEMED LIKE the whole world exploded. There was gunfire from battleships, destroyers, and cruisers. The bombers were still hitting the beaches. As we went in, we could see small craft from the 116th Infantry that had gone in ahead, sunk. There were bodies bobbing in the water, even out three or four miles.

Then there was a deep silence. All the gunfire had lifted; the Navy was giving way to let the troops get on the beaches. The sun was just coming up over the French coast. I saw a bird—a seagull, I guess—fly across the front of the boat, just like life was going on as normal.

Then there came something like a peppering of hail, heavy hail on the front of the ramp. I realized it was enemy machine-gun fire. All hell broke loose from the other side—

German artillery, rockets and mortars. It was just unbelievable that anyone could have lived under that barrage.

Our assault boat hit a sandbar. I looked over the ramp and we were at least seventy-five yards from the shore, and we had hoped for a dry landing. I told the coxswain, "Try to get in further." He screamed he couldn't. That British seaman had all the guts in the world but couldn't get off the sandbar. I told him to drop the ramp or we were going to die right there.

We had been trained for years not to go off the front of the ramp, because the boat might get rocked by a wave and run over you. So we went off the sides. I looked to my right and saw a B Company boat next to us with Lt. Bob Fitzsimmons, a good friend, take a direct hit on the ramp from a mortar or mine. I thought, there goes half of B Company.

It was cold, miserably cold, even though it was June. The water temperature was probably forty-five or fifty degrees. It was up to my shoulders when I went in, and I saw men sinking all about me. I tried to grab a couple, but my job was to get on in and get to the guns. There were bodies from the 116th floating everywhere. They were face-down in the water with packs still on their backs. They had inflated their life jackets. Fortunately, most of the Rangers did not inflate theirs or they also might have turned over and drowned.

I began to run with my rifle in front of me. I went directly across the beach to try to get to the seaway In front of me was part of the 116th Infantry, pinned down and lying behind beach obstacles. They hadn't made it to the seaway. I kept screaming at them, "You have to get up and go! You gotta get up and go!" But they didn't. They were worn out and defeated completely. There wasn't any time to help them.

I continued across the beach. There were mines and obstacles all up and down the beach. The air corps had missed it entirely. There were no shell holes in which to take cover. The mines had not been detonated. Absolutely nothing that had been planned for that part of the beach had worked. I knew that Vierville-sur-Mer was going to be a hellhole, and it was. ✷

LEFT:
The Last Full Measure
by Richard M. Gibney, 1991.
U.S. Marine Corps Museum,
Washington, D.C.

FOLLOWING PAGES:
Red Beach at Gela, 1700, July 10
by Mitchell Jamieson, 1943.

The Beach at Dusk by Mitchell Jamieson, 1945.

Iwo Jima

EDGAR L. JONES

American troops landed at Iwo Jima on February 19, 1945. The famous flag-raising on Mount Suribachi occurred on February 23, and by March 16 the island was under American control. Edgar L. Jones was an ambulance driver with the British Eighth Army in Africa before illness forced him from service. He saw action again as a correspondent in the Pacific for The Atlantic Monthly.

NO ONE WHO WAS AT IWO can analyze the battle objectively. The carnage was so horrifying that the blood and agony of the struggle saturated one's mind, dismally coloring all thought. Iwo was unlike any war I had ever seen. It was a fight to the finish, with no man asking for quarter until he was dead. Of the nearly 20,000 American casualties, approximately two thirds were wounded, but all except a few score of the 20,000 Japanese died where they fell. There is such a thing as dying decently, but not on Iwo. I do not believe anything practical can be achieved by describing men blown apart. Veterans of two and three years of war in the Pacific were sickened. An estimated 26,000 men died in eight square miles of fighting. There were 5,000 dead and wounded American and Japanese soldiers for every square mile.

I returned to Iwo on D-Day plus six, seven and eight. By that time the Marines had captured territory where Japanese had lain dead in the hot sun for more than a week. I crawled into pillboxes burned out by flame-throwers, and into deep caves where the Japanese had been burning their own dead to conceal the extent of their losses. I was torturing myself to look at the results of war, because I think it is essential for civilians occasionally to hold their noses and see what is going on.

The sight on Iwo which I could not force myself to see again was the section of the beach allotted for an American cemetery.... On the afternoon I walked by, there was half an acre of dead Marines stretched out so close together that they blanketed the beach for two hundred yards. The stench was overpowering.... The smell of one's countrymen rotting in the sun is a lasting impression. ✶

OPPOSITE:
Detail from *Solitaire Enroute Noumea* by David Fredenthal, 1943.

From

KING RAT

JAMES CLAVELL

Clavell, who served in the Royal Artillery, was captured on Java in 1942 and made a POW in the notorious Changi prison in Singapore.

A LONG TIME AGO the camp had started a university. The University of Changi. Classes were organized. The Brass had ordered it. "Good for the troops," they had said. "Give them something to do. *Make* them better themselves. *Force* them to be busy, then they won't get into trouble."

There were courses in languages and art and engineering—for among the original hundred thousand men there was at least one man who knew any subject.

The knowledge of the world. A great opportunity. Broaden horizons. Learn a trade. Prepare for the utopia that would come to pass once the goddam war ended and things were back to normal. And the university was Athenian. No classrooms. Only a teacher who found a place in the shade and grouped his students around him.

But the prisoners of Changi were just ordinary men, so they sat on their butts and said, "Tomorrow I'll join a class." Or they joined and when they discovered that knowledge comes hard they would miss a class and another class and then they would say, "Tomorrow I'll rejoin. Tomorrow I'll start to become what I want to be afterwards. Mustn't waste time. Tomorrow I'll really start."

But in Changi, as elsewhere, there was only today.

"You really want to join my class?" Vexley repeated incredulously.

"You sure we won't be putting you to any trouble, sir?" the King asked cordially.

Vexley got up with quickening interest and made a space for them in the shade.

He was delighted to see new blood. And the King! My God, what a catch! The King in *his* class! Maybe he'll have some cigarettes . . . "Delighted, my boy, delighted." He shook the King's extended hand warmly. "Squadron Leader Vexley!"

"Happy to know you, sir."

"Flight Lieutenant Marlowe," Peter Marlowe said as he also shook hands and sat down in the shade.

Vexley waited nervously till they were seated and absently pressed his thumb into the back of his hand, counting the seconds till the indentation in the skin slowly filled. Pellagra had its compensations, he thought. And thinking of skin and bone reminded him of whales and his pop-eye brightened. "Well, today I was going to talk about whales. Do you know about whales?—Ah," he said ecstatically as the King brought out a pack of Kooas and offered him one. The King passed the pack around the whole class.

The four students accepted the cigarettes and moved to give the King and Peter Marlowe more space. They wondered what

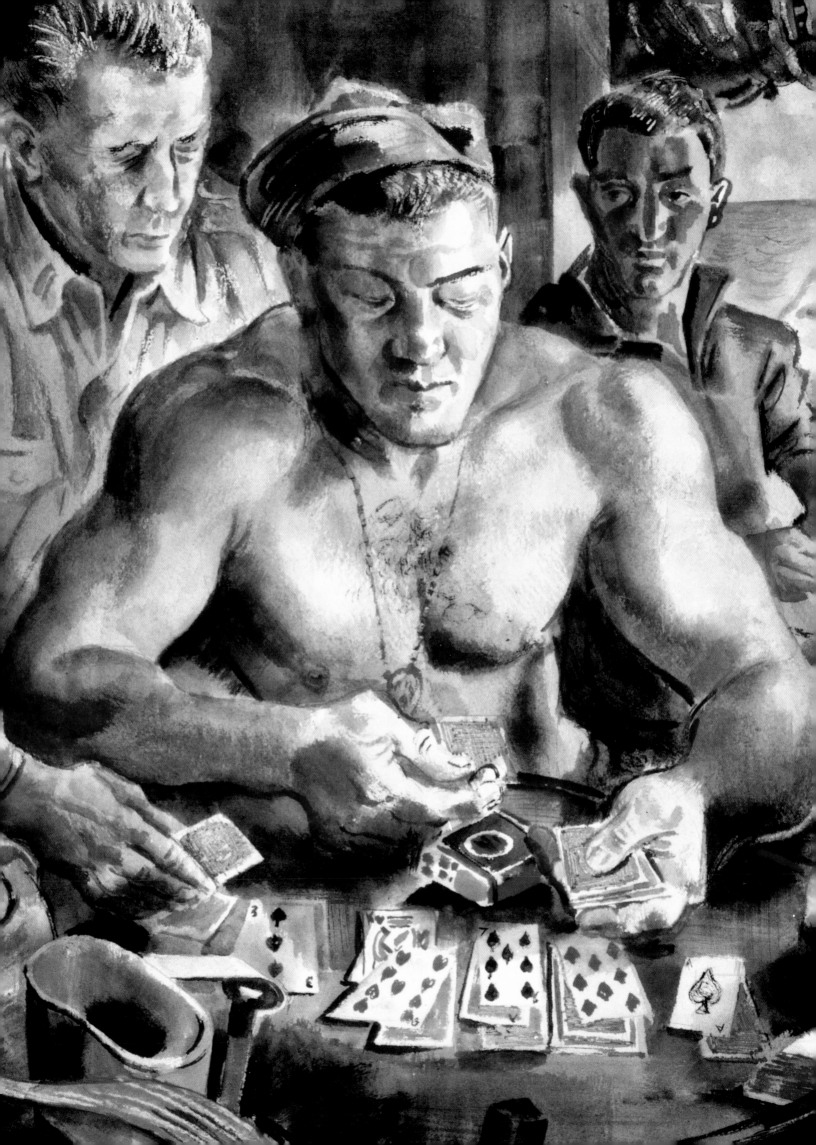

Limbless Officers and Men Checking out for Changi Gaol by Leslie Cole, 1945. Imperial War Museum, London.

the hell the King was doing there, but they didn't really care—he'd given them a real tailor-made cigarette.

Vexley started to continue his lecture on whales. He loved whales. He loved them to distraction.

"Whales are without a doubt the highest form that nature has aspired to," he said, very pleased with the resonance of his voice. He noticed the King's frown. "Did you have a question?" he asked eagerly.

"Well, yes. Whales are interesting, but what about rats?"

"I beg your pardon," Vexley said politely.

"Very interesting what you were saying about whales, sir," the King said. "I was just wondering about rats, that's all."

"What about rats?"

"I was just wondering if you knew anything about them," the King said. He had a lot to do and didn't want to screw around.

"What he means," Peter Marlowe said

quickly, "is that if whales are almost human in their reflexes, isn't that true of rats, too?"

Vexley shook his head and said distastefully, "Rodents are entirely different. Now about whales . . ."

"How are they different?" asked the King.

"I cover the rodents in the spring seminar," Vexley said testily. "Disgusting beasts. Nothing about them to like. Nothing. Now you take the sulphur-bottom whale," Vexley hastily launched off again. "Ah, now there's the giant of all whales. Over a hundred feet long and it can weigh as much as a hundred and fifty tons. The biggest creature alive—that has ever lived—on earth. The most powerful animal in existence. And its mating habits," Vexley added quickly, for he knew that a discussion of the sex life always kept the class awake.

"Its mating is marvelous. The male begins his titillation by blowing glorious clouds of spray. He pounds the water with his tail near the female, who waits with patient lust on the ocean's surface. Then he will dive deep and soar up, out of the water, huge, vast, enormous, and crash back with thundering flukes, churning the water into foam, pounding at the surface." He dropped his voice sensuously. "Then he slides up to the female and starts tickling her with his flippers . . ."

In spite of his anxiety about rats, even the King began to listen attentively.

"Then he will break off the seduction and dive again, leaving the female panting on the surface—leaving her perhaps for good." Vexley made a dramatic pause. "But no. He doesn't leave her. He disappears for perhaps an hour, into the depths of the ocean, gathering strength, and then he soars up once more and bursts clear of the water and falls like a clap of thunder in a monstrous cloud of spray. He whirls over and over onto his mate, hugging her tight with both flippers and has his mighty will of her to exhaustion."

Vexley was exhausted, too, at the magnificence of the spectacle of mating giants. Ah, to be so lucky as to witness it, to be there, an insignificant human . . .

He rushed on: "Mating takes place about July, in warm waters. The baby weighs five tons at birth and is about thirty feet long." His laugh was practiced. "Think of that." There were polite smiles, and then Vexley came in with the clincher, always good for a deep chuckle. "And if you think of that and the size of the calf, just think about the whale's jolly old John Thomas, what?" Again there were courteous smiles—the regular members had heard the story many times.

Vexley went on to describe how the calf is nursed for seven months by the mother, who supplies the calf with milk from two monstrous teats toward the ass end of her underside. "As you can no doubt imagine," he said ecstatically, "prolonged suckling underwater has its problems."

"Do rats suckle their young?" The King jumped in quickly.

"Yes," the squadron leader said miserably. "Now about ambergris . . ."

The King sighed, beaten, and listened to Vexley expound about ambergris and sperm whales and toothed whales and white whales and goose-beaked whales and pygmy whales and beaked whales and narwhales and killer whales and humpback whales and bottle-nosed whales and whalebone whales and gray whales and right whales and finally bowhead whales. By this time all the class except Peter Marlowe and the King had left. When Vexley had finished, the King said simply:

"I want to know about rats."

Vexley groaned. "Rats?"

"Have a cigarette," said the King benignly.

———

"ALL RIGHT, YOU GUYS, sort yourselves out," the King said. He waited until there was quiet in the hut and the lookout at the doorway was in position. "We got problems."

"Grey?" asked Max.

"No. It's about our farm." The King turned to Peter Marlowe, who was sitting on the edge of a bed. "You tell 'em, Peter."

"Well," began Peter Marlowe, "it seems that rats—"

"Tell 'em it from the beginning."

"All of it?"

"Sure. Spread the knowledge, then we can all figure angles."

"All right. Well, we found Vexley. He told us, quote: 'The *Rattus norvegicus*, or Norwegian rat—sometimes called the *Mus decumanus*—'"

"What sort of talk is that?" Max asked.

"Latin, for Chrissake. Any fool knows that," Tex said.

"You know Latin, Tex?" Max gaped at him.

"Hell no, but those crazy names're always Latin—"

"For Chrissake, you guys," the King said. "You want to know or don't you?" Then he nodded for Peter Marlowe to continue.

"Well, anyway, Vexley described them in detail, hairy, no hair on the tail, weight up to four pounds, the usual is about two pounds in this part of the world. Rats mate promiscuously at any time—"

"What the hell does that mean?"

"The male'll screw any female irrespective," the King said impatiently, "and there ain't no season."

"Just like us, you mean?" Jones said agreeably.

"Yes. I suppose so," said Peter Marlowe. "Anyway, the male rat will mate at any season and the female can have up to twelve litters per year, around twelve per litter, but perhaps as many as fourteen. The young are born blind and helpless twenty-two days after—contact." He picked the word delicately. "The young open their eyes after fourteen to seventeen days and become sexually mature in two months. They cease

Washing by George Biddle, 1943. Courtesy D. Wigmore Fine Art, Inc., NY.

breeding at about two years and are old at three years."

"Holy cow!" Max said delightedly in the awed silence. "We sure as hell've problems. Why, if the young'll breed in two months, and we get twelve—say for round figures ten a litter—figure it for yourself. Say we get ten young on Day One. Another ten on Day Thirty. By Day Sixty the first five pair've bred, and we get fifty. Day Ninety we got another five pairs breeding and another fifty. Day One-twenty, we got two-fifty plus another fifty and another fifty and a new batch of two-fifty. For Chrissake, that makes six-fifty in five months. The next month we got near six thousand five hundred—"

"Jesus, we got us a gold mine!" Miller said, scratching furiously.

"The hell we have," the King said. "Not without some figuring. Number one, we can't put 'em all together. They're cannibals. That means we got to separate the males and females except when we're mating them. Another thing, they'll fight among themselves, all the time. So that means separating males from males and females from females."

"So we separate them. What's so tough about that?"

"Nothing, Max," said the King patiently. "But we got to have cages and get the thing organized. It isn't going to be easy."

"Hell," Tex said. "We can build a stock of cages, no sweat in that."

"You think, Tex, we can keep the farm quiet? While we're building up the stock?"

"Don't see why not!"

"Oh, another thing," the King said. He was feeling pleased with the men and more than pleased with the scheme. It was a business after his own heart—nothing to do except wait. "They'll eat anything, alive or dead. Anything. So we've no logistics problem."

"But they're filthy creatures and they'll stink to the skies," Byron Jones III said. "We've enough stench around here as it is without putting more under our own hut. And rats are also plague carriers!"

"Maybe that's a special type of rat, like a special mosquito carries malaria," Dino said hopefully, his dark eyes roving the men.

"Rats can carry plague, sure," the King said, shrugging. "And they carry a lot of human diseases. But that don't mean nothing. We got a fortune in the making and all you bastards do is figure negatives! It's un-American!"

"Well, Jesus, this plague bit. How do we know if they'll be clean or not?" Miller said queasily.

The King laughed. "We asked Vexley that an' he said, quote, 'You'd find out soon enough. You'd be dead.' Unquote. Hell, it's just like chickens. Keep 'em clean and feed 'em good and you got good stock! Nothing to worry about."

So they talked about the farm, its dangers and its potentials—and they could all appreciate the potentials—provided they *didn't* have to eat the produce—and they discussed the problems connected with such a large-scale operation. Then Kurt came into the hut and in his hands was a squirming blanket.

"I got another," he said sourly.

"You have?"

"Sure I have. While you bastards're talkin' I'm out doin'. It's a bitch." Kurt spat on the floor.

"How do you know?"

"I looked. I seed enough rats in the Merchant Marine to know. An' the other's a male. An' I looked too."

They all climbed under the hut and watched Kurt put Eve into the trench. Immediately the two rats stuck together viciously, and the men were hard put not to cheer. The first litter was on its way. The men

voted that Kurt was to be in charge and Kurt was happy.

That way he knew he would get his share. Sure he'd look after the rats. Food was food. Kurt knew he was going to survive if any bastard did.

———

TWENTY-TWO DAYS LATER Eve gave birth. In the next cage, Adam tore at the wire netting to get at the living food and almost got through, but Tex spotted the rent just in time. Eve suckled the young. There were Cain and Abel and Grey and Alliluha; Beulah and Mabel and Junt and Princess and Little Princess and Big Mabel and Big Junt and Big Beulah. Naming the males was easy. But none of the men wanted their girls' names or their sisters' or their mothers' names attached to the females. Even mother-in-law names were some other man's passion or relation of the past. It had taken them three days to agree on Beulah and Mabel.

When the young were fifteen days old, they were put into separate cages. The King, Peter Marlowe, Tex and Max gave Eve until noon to recover, then put her back with Adam. The second litter was launched.

"Peter," the King said benignly as they climbed through the trapdoor into the hut, "our fortune's made." ✷

———

Changi was not even the worst Japanese camp. POWs on forced-labor projects, such as the Burma-Thailand Railway, actually suffered conditions that were more harsh, with slimmer odds of survival.

v. HUMANITY

REVERENCE WAS PUT TO THE TEST as soon as bombs struck. One of the first hit songs of the war was Frank Loesser's "Praise the Lord and Pass the Ammunition." Its title and chorus were taken from a line credited to Howell Maurice Forgy, a chaplain—"sky pilot" in the song—aboard the cruiser *New Orleans* during the attack on Pearl Harbor:

Down went the gunner, a bullet was his fate
Down went the gunner, and then the gunner's mate
Up jumped the sky pilot, gave the boys a look
And manned the gun himself as he laid aside The Book,
    shouting . . .

Praise the Lord and pass the ammunition
Praise the Lord and pass the ammunition
Praise the Lord and pass the ammunition
And we'll all stay free

The sky pilot may have seen no conflict between the call to God and the call to arms, but not everyone was so self-assured. First Lady Eleanor Roosevelt took the step of addressing that question directly in a magazine article titled "Must We Hate to Fight?" Eventually the war's brutality challenged the faith of even passionate believers. Many of the soldiers and sailors who witnessed genocide and possessed the first weapons of mass destruction found it difficult to believe in their Sunday school lessons of God's omnipotence. Instead, they were humbled and confused by the very might they now possessed. (Is it any surprise that Jean-Paul Sartre wrote *Being and Nothingness,* the bible of existentialism, during the Nazi occupation of France?) Nonetheless, faith did not disappear. The determination to survive made each person face the difficulty of remaining human during an inhuman war. A new kind of reverence filled the places where old beliefs had been. Small pets really were coddled like children, just like in the movies. Battle-hardened soldiers painstakingly labored in gardens. And everyone had a story about a heartening moment—a chance meeting of old friends, or a few minutes with someone unforgettable. A telling phrase is credited to William Thomas Cummings, from a field sermon on Bataan in 1942: "There are no atheists in the foxholes."

"The suffering of the men left a mark from which I think I shall never be free."

—ELEANOR ROOSEVELT, following a tour of the Pacific Theater of Operations

MUST WE HATE TO FIGHT?

ELEANOR ROOSEVELT

On July 4, 1942, the first Independence Day after Pearl Harbor, the First Lady asked Americans a simple but weighty question in the popular magazine The Saturday Review.

CAN WE KILL OTHER HUMAN BEINGS if we do not hate them? I suppose the answer must come from those in our fighting forces. Some young people will tell you that unless you hate the people of Germany and Japan, you cannot possibly win. On the other hand, many a young soldier going into the war will assure you that he cannot hate the individuals of any race. He can only hate the system that has made those individuals his enemies. If he must kill them in order to do away with the system, he will do so, but not because he hates them as individuals. If those who say that to win the war we must hate, are really expressing the beliefs of the majority of our people, I am afraid we have already lost the peace, because our main objective is to make a world in which all the people of the world may live with respect and good will for each other in peace.

If we allow the hate of other men as individuals to possess us, we cannot discard hate the day we have won and suddenly become understanding and co-operative neighbors.

There will be no victory if out of this war we simply develop armed camps again throughout the world. We may in the interests of self-preservation cut down the actual race to obtain gulls, planes, and battleships because no people will survive if it goes on, nor will those who survive have the wherewithal for the decencies of life. Even if we cut out all weapons of force, there can exist armed camps in the minds of people, which express themselves through the economic systems that we set up and through all the barriers that we set up between peoples to keep them from real understanding. If we really do not mean that after this war we intend to see that people the world over have an opportunity to obtain a satisfactory life, then all we are doing is to prepare for a new war. There is no excuse for the bloodshed, the sacrifices, and the tears that the world as a whole is now enduring, unless we build a new worthwhile world.

The saving grace for most of us is that hope does spring eternal in the human breast. We do believe that just around the corner is the solution to our problems that we have long been looking for, and that human beings will never give up till they find the answers.

Prisoners Digging Graves by Mitchell Jamieson, 1944.

I believe that the solution will be easier to find when we work together, and when all the plans, all the abilities of people the world over, are concentrated on finding positive solutions, but if we hate each other then I despair of achieving any ultimate good results.

I will acknowledge that it is easier to urge upon our people that they hate those whom we now must fight as individuals, because it is always easier to build up contempt and dislike for that which is making us suffer than it is to force ourselves to analyze the reasons that have brought about these conditions and try to eliminate them.

In small ways we see over and over again that the child who is badgered and punished in youth grows up to treat anyone weaker than himself in much the same way. That is probably what we will do to the people of our nation as a whole when we tell them that in fighting to stamp out cruelty and hate, dominated by force, they must hate. Somehow as a whole the thousands in our fighting forces must preserve a belief and a respect for the individual and a hate only of the system, or else we will go down ourselves, victims of the very system that today we are striving to conquer. ✳

CAPTAIN WASKOW

ERNIE PYLE

Pyle, a syndicated columnist for Scripps-Howard, was probably the nation's favorite war correspondent. This 1943 report, for which he won a Pulitzer Prize, is his most famous. When victory in Europe became a foregone conclusion, Pyle went to the Pacific. He was killed on April 18, 1945, landing with troops on a small island near Okinawa.

FRONTLINES IN ITALY—In this war I have known a lot of officers who were loved and respected by the soldiers under them. But never have I crossed the trail of any man as beloved as Capt. Henry T. Waskow, of Belton, Texas.

Captain Waskow was a company commander in the 36th Division. He had led his company since long before it left the States. He was very young, only in his middle 20's, but he carried in him a sincerity and a gentleness that made people want to be guided by him.

"After my own father, he came next," a sergeant told me.

"He always looked after us," a soldier said. "He'd go to bat for us every time."

"I've never known him to do anything unfair," another one said.

I was at the foot of the mule trail the night they brought Capt. Waskow's body down the mountain. The moon was nearly full at the time, and you could see far up the trail, and even part way across the valley. Soldiers made shadows as they walked.

Dead men had been coming down the mountain all evening, lashed onto the backs of mules. They came lying belly-down across wooden pack saddles—their heads hanging down on the left side of the mule, their stiffened legs sticking out awkwardly from the other side, bobbing up and down as the mule walked.

The Italian mule-skinners were afraid to walk beside dead men, so Americans had to lead the mules down that night. Even the Americans were reluctant to unlash and lift off the bodies at the bottom, so an officer had to do it himself, and ask others to help.

The first one came early in the evening. They slid him down from the mule and stood him on his feet for a moment. In the half-light he might have been merely a sick man standing there, leaning on the others. Then they lay him on the ground in the shadow of the low stone wall alongside the road.

I don't know who that first one was. You feel small in the presence of the dead men, and ashamed at being alive, and you don't ask silly questions.

We left him there beside the road, that first one, and we all went back into the cowshed and sat on water cans or lay on the straw, waiting for the next batch of mules.

Somebody said the dead soldier had been dead for four days, and then nobody said anything more about it. We talked soldier talk for an hour or more. The dead man lay all alone outside, in the shadow of the stone wall.

Then a soldier came into the dark cowshed and said there were some more bodies outside. We went out into the road. Four mules stood there, in the moonlight, in the road where the trail came down off the mountain. The soldiers who led them stood there waiting. "This one is Capt. Waskow," one of them said quietly.

Two men unlashed his body from the mule and lifted it off and lay it in the shadow beside the low stone wall. Other men took the other bodies off. Finally there were five,

lying end to end in a long row alongside the road. You don't cover up dead men in the combat zone. They just lie there in the shadows until somebody else comes after them.

The unburdened mules moved off to their olive orchard. The men in the road seemed reluctant to leave. They stood around, and gradually one by one you could sense them moving close to Capt. Waskow's body. Not so much to look, I think, as to say something in finality, to him and to themselves. I stood close by and I could hear. One soldier came and looked down and he said out loud, "Goddammit." That's all he said, and then he walked away. Another one came. He said "Goddammit to hell anyway." He looked down for a few moments, and then he turned and left.

Another man came; I think he was an officer. It was hard to tell officers from men in the half-light, for all were bearded and grimy dirty. The man looked down into the dead captain's face, and then he spoke directly to him, as though he were alive. He said:

"I'm sorry, old man."

Then a soldier came and stood beside the officer, and bent over, and he too spoke to his dead captain, not in a whisper but awfully tenderly, and he said:

"I sure am sorry, sir."

Then the first man squatted down, and he reached down and took the dead hand, and he sat there for five full minutes, holding the dead hand in his own and looking intently into the dead face, and he never uttered a sound all the time he sat there.

And then finally he put the hand down, and then reached up and gently straightened the points of the captain's shirt collar, and then he sort of rearranged the tattered edges of his uniform around the wound. And then he got up and walked away down the road in the moonlight, all alone. ✴

Last Rites for the Sergeant by Kerr Eby, 1944.

She Was Toronto, She Was Home

from Barry Broadfoot's
Six War Years: 1939–1945

ANONYMOUS

IT'S FUNNY THE THINGS YOU REMEMBER, but I can remember one weekend clearly. This one just stays and stays in my mind and I can still be driving down the highway or mowing the lawn and suddenly there it is. It is just a weekend I spent with a CWAC in London. She was a girl I'd known at Collegiate [high school] in Toronto. I can't say I ever knew her well in high school or that I got to know her much better that weekend, but it is the one single memory I remember.

It was April 1944. I'd been on those big raids to Berlin and poor godforsaken Hamburg, which had been hit about three times by every single plane in Bomber Command. And then I get a 72-hour pass and I'm off to London.

I get in to Victoria Station about eleven in the morning and I slope off to my usual hotel in Ecclestone Square, and the old granny who ran it was glad to see me. A quid for the weekend, and she used to laugh and say, "I close my eyes and I sleep sound after pub closing, Canada," meaning, of course, what we did after that, she didn't care about. With girls, I mean. Women. London was full of them.

I wandered around. Along the Embank-ment. Into the Tate. Over to Trafalgar Square, to that madhouse of thousands of troops, sailors, airmen, girls, young and old. Into the National Gallery. Up to Piccadilly. Finding a pub open and having two or three pints and a bun. Just another airman on leave in a big town and not knowing anyone. God, but it is a lonely feeling, and I just wasn't one to make friends with some Yank or Aussie or hunt up some Canadian in a bar and make conversation.

And then I saw her. In Trafalgar Square, just standing on the steps there by the lions and I remember yelling, "Smitty!" and she spotted my arm waving and then my face, and she ran down the steps and into my arms. I can remember it now. Here was Smitty in London, a girl I'd gone to school with in Toronto, gone to Centre Island with on a picnic once, and with the class on a picnic up the Don Valley once. You know. She was in the army, a CWAC, and on leave. I can see her now. She wasn't a good-looking girl, but she did have an interesting face, lots of freckles and what you'd call a sardonic smile. I remember at school she had this dry wit. That's the only way I can describe it. She was tall, almost as tall as I was, and what you might call skinny. She wasn't pretty, but how many beautiful girls did you see in the service? Not many. But she had something.

And she was more. She was Toronto, she was home. She was talk, and she was a friend and she was fun and she knew the people I knew and, above all, she was home and I needed a good dash of home right then.

We became lovers immediately. Nothing was said. I didn't ask her if she had a date that night with the King of England. We were just lovers, and if I wanted to pay her a quid I'd buy her whiskey or dinner and not hand it over, as you did and have the tart stuff it in her handbag and pat you on the cheek and say, "Ta, ta, luv. Till we meet again." She wasn't a whore, she was a girl from Toronto and we'd met in London among six million people. We'd found each other.

There was something about England, London, that spring. Everybody knew the invasion was coming and it was kind of like a time, I suppose, when England knew the Spanish Armada was coming and everybody was excited.

We went to pubs, we went to dinner and we strolled through Green Park and looked at the children with their nannies and then we went down to Ecclestone Park and I boosted her over the fence. The park is locked, you know. It's for residents of the area. I think there was a vegetable garden in part of it, but we walked under the trees and then we went home, up three flights of narrow stairs, into that bedroom and we made love. I mean we really made love. This just wasn't a screw. And next morning old granny brought us our breakfast in bed, the lovable old sot.

Saturday we did the same, walked around, went to a picture show. *Mrs. Miniver.* Greer Garson. Britain at war. What a phony. You could hear the people muttering all around, making rude remarks about Greer Garson's clothes. Nobody dressed like that in Britain any more. We went out to Kew and then down into the East End to one of those singing pubs and we went back and made love, and then went out and spent an evening in a local, drinking beer and playing darts, and then we made love again and next morning too. You see, I can remember it all.

That afternoon she put me on the five o'clock train for my station in Kent and I kissed her out of the compartment window just like you used to see in old war movies, and that's the last I saw of her. We wrote a bit, saying we'd see each other back in Canada because the invasion was coming up fast by then, but we never did.

It was my fault, I guess. She didn't blame me, in her letters. It was just, I felt, that in those three days we had done everything we would have wanted to do for the rest of our lives or, anyway, for the rest of the war. And so it was enough. I felt that way, and she did too, I think. It was our own private and special wartime marriage. ✻

Night Travelers by Lieutenant T. R. MacDonald, 1943. Canadian War Museum, Ottawa.

Landscape of the Vernal Equinox by Paul Nash, 1944. © Tate, London 2001.

ENCHANTMENT

GREGORY CLARK

Gregory Clark, a veteran of the First World War, was already a well-known reporter before covering the Second World War for the Toronto Star. *After the war, he became one of the country's most popular columnists.*

IN 1924, HARRY PLUNKET GREENE, a famous British concert singer, wrote a book called *Where the Bright Waters Meet.*

I got my first copy in 1925. In 1925-6-7-8-9 I must have bought twelve or fifteen copies, as fast as my friends and colleagues stole, pinched or mislaid them. It was a book about a little river, three miles long, called the Bourne, in the south of England; and a tiny village, Hurstbourne Priors. There are those who believe the book to be perhaps the greatest literary expression of the magic spell, the psyche, of fly fishing. At any rate, in my mind and heart, the Bourne and Hurstbourne Priors moved long ago into the special sanctuary where

Tintagel is kept, and the dark tower to which Childe Roland came.

In June, 1944, I was in the Sausage Machine. This was the name given to that gigantic march of a million young men down to the sea and over to Normandy to put an end to a world terror. In fiercely-guarded secrecy, we were moved in our truck convoys from all parts of Britain down to Portsmouth and all the exits where the landing ships waited. I was with an Air Force unit. Already in my fifties, my blue battle dress ill-becoming my potty form, my white side-whiskers incongruous under the little wedge cap, this war correspondent cut a poor figure amidst all those glorious young men. It was when we bailed out of our lorries at one of the desperately-secret staging camps en route to the sea that I felt most inappropriate to that great hour and scene.

The staging camp was merely a bare hill, trodden by those who had already gone before us: a few huts, some tents. Our lorries were parked. A British army major in command of the camp—tall, lean, hard, grim—addressed us and warned us not to attempt to set foot outside the confines of the camp. The boys dispersed to the huts, the tents.

This major, standing apart on the bare field, was the familiar type: cold, malign, his blue eyes bleakly observing, his attitude stiff, remote. It is a type I have always detested. But in me there is some imp or devil that has ever pushed me to walk up and approach those who repel me. I walked over to the major.

"Could you tell me," I asked easily, "what is that steeple in the distance there?"

Against the gray late afternoon sky, far off, a spire lifted gloriously.

The major eyed me with a mixture of curiosity and disdain. As I say, I was not a prepossessing figure.

"That is Salisbury," he replied drily.

I looked to the left. A river glinted in the distant valley.

"And that river?"

"The Test," said the major.

I glanced down the hill on which we stood, over the meadows, the woods, and close in was a little stream, to be seen in bits and pieces.

I felt an electric thrill steal up my spine, and burst like a tiny rocket amidst my back hair.

"And this small stream?" I said, a little hoarsely, for it flowed into The Test.

"The Bourne," said the major.

With difficulty, I withdrew my eyes from the valley and raised them to the cold eyes of the major.

"Where the Bright Waters Meet," I said.

A weird thing happened. It was as if something hot boiled behind the eyes of the major; his gaze faltered, melted.

"You know it?" he asked.

"Harry Plunket Greene," I said, in testimony.

The major turned to stand beside me.

"Hurstbourne Priors," he said, "is beyond those trees, a park. I would rather you did not go that far. Go down the hill, here. I'll signal the sentry. The path will take you to that farm house. You see its roof? My rod is over the mantel; the woman will give it to you. You will have to moisten the leader, there is a fly mounted . . ."

"Iron blue?" I asked, for that would have to be the fly.

"Yes," said the major.

I went down the hill, got the rod, knelt in the watercress while the leader moistened; saw the trout dimpling; cast and caught three; stuffed them with sedge grass in my battle dress blouse, put the rod back in the farm house.

And the major and I ate them alone, for supper, and talked about Plunket Greene. The order presently came; and the young men piled into their lorries; and we went on down to the sea. ✱

Detail from *The Hitler Line*
by Charles Comfort, 1944.
Canadian War Museum, Ottawa.

From

SLAUGHTERHOUSE-FIVE

KURT VONNEGUT

BILLY WAS A CHAPLAIN'S ASSISTANT in the war. A chaplain's assistant is customarily a figure of fun in the American Army. Billy was no exception. He was powerless to harm the enemy or to help his friends. In fact, he had no friends. He was a valet to a preacher, expected no promotions or medals, bore no arms, and had a meek faith in a loving Jesus which most soldiers found putrid.

While on maneuvers in South Carolina, Billy played hymns he knew from childhood, played them on a little black organ which was waterproof. It had thirty-nine keys and two stops—*vox humana* and *vox celeste*. Billy also had charge of a portable altar, an olive-drab attaché case with telescoping legs. It was lined with crimson plush, and nestled in that passionate plush were an anodized aluminum cross and a Bible.

The altar and the organ were made by a vacuum cleaner company in Camden, New Jersey—and said so.

ONE TIME ON MANEUVERS Billy was playing "A Mighty Fortress Is Our God," with music by Johann Sebastian Bach and words by Martin Luther. It was Sunday morning. Billy and his chaplain had gathered a congregation of about fifty soldiers on a Carolina hillside. An umpire appeared. There were umpires everywhere, men who said who was winning or losing the theoretical battle, who was alive and who was dead.

The umpire had comical news. The congregation had been theoretically spotted from the air by a theoretical enemy. They were all theoretically dead now. The theoretical corpses laughed and ate a hearty noontime meal.

Remembering this incident years later, Billy was struck by what a Tralfamadorian adventure with death that had been, to be dead and to eat at the same time.

Toward the end of maneuvers, Billy was given an emergency furlough home because his father, a barber in Ilium, New York, was shot dead by a friend while they were out hunting deer. So it goes.

WHEN BILLY GOT BACK from his furlough, there were orders for him to go overseas. He was needed in the headquarters company of an infantry regiment fighting in Luxembourg. The regimental chaplain's assistant had been killed in action. So it goes.

When Billy joined the regiment, it was in the process of being destroyed by the Germans in the famous Battle of the Bulge. Billy never even got to meet the chaplain he was supposed to assist, was never even issued a steel helmet and combat boots. This was in December of 1944, during the last mighty German attack of the war.

Billy survived, but he was a dazed wanderer far behind the new German lines. Three other wanderers, not quite so dazed, allowed Billy to tag along. Two of them were scouts, and one was an antitank gunner. They were without food or maps. Avoiding Germans, they were delivering themselves into rural silences ever more profound. They ate snow.

They went Indian file. First came the scouts, clever, graceful, quiet. They had rifles. Next came the antitank gunner, clumsy and dense, warning Germans away with a Colt .45 automatic in one hand and a trench knife in the other.

Last came Billy Pilgrim, empty-handed, bleakly ready for death. Billy was preposterous—six feet and three inches tall, with a chest and shoulders like a box of kitchen matches. He had no helmet, no overcoat, no weapon, and no boots. On his feet were cheap, low-cut civilian shoes which he had bought for his father's funeral. Billy had lost a heel, which made him bob up-and-down, up-and-down. The involuntary dancing, up-and-down, up-and-down, made his hip joints sore.

Billy was wearing a thin field jacket, a shirt and trousers of scratchy wool, and long underwear that was soaked with sweat. He was the only one of the four who had a beard. It was a random, bristly beard, and some of the bristles were white, even though Billy was only twenty-one years old. He was also going bald. Wind and cold and violent exercise had turned his face crimson.

He didn't look like a soldier at all. He looked like a filthy flamingo.

AND ON THE THIRD DAY of wandering, somebody shot at the four from far away—shot four times as they crossed a narrow brick road. One shot was for the scouts. The next one was for the antitank gunner, whose name was Roland Weary.

The third bullet was for the filthy flamingo, who stopped dead center in the road when the lethal bee buzzed past his ear. Billy stood there politely, giving the marksman another chance. It was his addled understanding of the rules of warfare that the marksman *should* be given a second chance. The next shot missed Billy's kneecaps by inches, going end-on-end, from the sound of it.

Roland Weary and the scouts were safe in a ditch, and Weary growled at Billy, "Get out of the road, you dumb motherfucker." The last word was still a novelty in the speech of white people in 1944. It was fresh and astonishing to Billy, who had never fucked anybody—and it did its job. It woke him up and got him off the road.

"SAVED YOUR LIFE AGAIN, you dumb bastard," Weary said to Billy in the ditch. He had been saving Billy's life for days, cursing him, kicking him, slapping him, making him move. It was absolutely necessary that cruelty be used, because Billy wouldn't do anything to save himself. Billy wanted to quit. He was cold, hungry, embarrassed, incompetent. He could scarcely distinguish between sleep and wakefulness now, on the third day, found no important differences, either, between walking and standing still.

He wished everybody would leave him alone. "You guys go on without me," he said again and again.

he had helped to fire one shot in anger— from a 57-millimeter antitank gun. The gun made a ripping sound like the opening of the zipper on the fly of God Almighty. The gun lapped up snow and vegetation with a blowtorch thirty feet long. The flame left a black arrow on the ground, showing the Germans exactly where the gun was hidden. The shot was a miss.

What had been missed was a Tiger tank. It swiveled its 88-millimeter snout around sniffingly, saw the arrow on the ground. It fired. It killed everybody on the gun crew but Weary. So it goes. ✶

WEARY WAS AS NEW TO WAR as Billy. He was a replacement, too. As a part of a gun crew,

Explosion by Tom Lea, 1942.

STILL FALLS THE RAIN

EDITH SITWELL

Still falls the Rain—
Dark as the world of man, black as our loss—
Blind as the nineteen hundred and forty nails
Upon the Cross.

Still falls the Rain
With a sound like the pulse of the heart that is changed to the hammer beat,
In the Potter's Field, and the sound of the impious feet

On the Tomb:
Still falls the Rain
In the Field of Blood where the small hopes breed and in the human brain
Nurtures its greed, that worm with the brow of Cain.

Still falls the Rain—
At the feet of the Starved Man hung upon the Cross.
Christ that each day, each night, nails there, have mercy on us—
On Dives and on Lazarus:
Under the Rain the sore and the gold are as one.

Still falls the Rain—
Still falls the Blood from the Starved Man's wounded Side:
He bears in His Heart all wounds,—those of the light that died,
The last faint spark
In the self-murdered heart, the wounds of the sad uncomprehending dark,

The wounds of the baited bear—
The blind and weeping bear whom the keepers beat
On his helpless flesh . . . the tears of the hunted hare.

Devastation in the City by Graham Sutherland, 1941. Imperial War Museum, London.

Still falls the Rain—
Then—O Ile leape up to my God: who pulles me doune—
See, see where Christ's blood streames in the firmament:
It flows from the Brow we nailed upon the tree
Deep to the dying, to the thirsting heart
That holds the fires of the world,—dark-smirched with pain
As Caesar's laurel crown.

Then sounds the voice of One who like the heart of man
Was once a child who among beasts has lain—
"Still do I love, still shed my innocent light, my Blood, for thee."

LETTERS HOME

THIS PAGE:
Tracy Sugarman, an ensign with
the United States Naval Reserve,
landed on Utah Beach during the
D-Day invasion.

RIGHT:
Army PFC Peter Sanfilippo fought on the Italian-North African front in the 633rd Field Artillery unit. His letters and paintings were sent home in empty bombshell canisters.

BELOW:
George Rarey, a captain in the 379th Fighter Squadron of the Army Air Corps, flew missions in England, and participated in the D-Day invasion. He was killed in action while flying a search-and-destroy mission in central France.

VI. MORALE

If it moves, salute it. If it doesn't move, pick it up. If you can't pick it up, paint it.

—"THE SAD SACK'S CATECHISM"

IN THE FIELD and on the home front, the irrationality of military life was an endless source of amusement. It's no coincidence that our buzzword for an absurd paradox—"Catch-22"—comes from a work of Second World War literature.

The humor was more than an indulgence; it diverted the country's attention, however briefly. It let GIs blow off steam about a system that was always bureaucratic, often muddled, and sometimes capable of a SNAFU that left men dead. As cartoonist Bill Mauldin's dogface Willie complained, "I feel like a fugitive from th' law of averages." That comment cuts two ways. Under some circumstances, wisecracks may have seemed inappropriate; but they beat the woeful alternatives.

Like the rest of the war, morale became an industrialized effort. Hollywood churned out features and shorts as propaganda. To entertain troops, the United Services Organization (USO) was created in early 1941 (when war seemed likely to many) by the YMCA, YWCA, National Catholic Community Service, National Jewish Welfare Board, Traveler's Aid Association, and Salvation Army. It established more than 3,000 centers in the United States over the next few years, and put on more than 400,000 shows between 1941 and 1947.

So, to the extent that war has a lighter side, here it is.

A portion of the 10,000 GI's who were on hand to witness the Copacabana All Girl Review at the Glenn Miller Theater, near Marseilles, France, 1945. Photo by Bransford (Army).

From See Here, Private Hargrove

MARION HARGROVE

*Hargrove's send-up of basic training at Fort Bragg, North Carolina,
became a best-selling book and a popular motion picture.*

"AND WHAT DID YOU DO in civil life?" my corporal asked me.

"I was feature editor of the Charlotte *News*."

"And just what sort of work did you do, Private Hargrove? Just give me a brief idea."

Seven minutes later, I had finished answering that question.

"Let's just put down here, 'Editorial worker.' He sighed compassionately. "And what did you do before all that?"

I told him. I brought in the publicity work, the soda-jerking, the theater ushering, and the printer's deviling.

"Private Hargrove," he said, "the Army is just what you have needed to ease the burdens of your existence. Look no farther, Private Hargrove, you have found a home."

THIS WAS A LOVELY MORNING. We began at daybreak and devoted all the time until noon to enjoying the beauties of nature. We had a drill sergeant to point them out to us. We marched a full twenty miles without leaving the drill field. Lunch, needless to say, was delicious.

We fell into bed, after lunch, determined to spend the afternoon in dreamland. Two minutes later, that infernal whistle blew. Melvin Piel, guardhouse lawyer for company A, explained it all on the way downstairs. We were going to be assigned to our permanent stations.

The sergeant called off the first list of names and the boys fell out. I heard him tell them that they were going to Virginia. "That's nothing," said Piel. "We're next, and we're going to California." Guardhouse Lawyer Piel smiled happily

The sergeant began the second list. "Moscowitz! Goldberg! Pinelli! Jones! Smith! Brown—" He stopped short. Then he started looking down the front line, choosing men to fill out the list. I smiled brightly from under my floppy denim cap at him.

"What's your name?" he asked.

"Hargrove, sir."

"Groves?"

"Hargrove, sir."

"All right, Grove. Fall in with those men over there."

I fell in and a corporal led us off down the street. I could feel the California palm trees fanning my face. We stopped at Barracks 17 and the corporal led us inside.

"Do we go to California, corporal?" I asked.

"Naah," he said.

"Where do we go?" I asked him, a little disappointed.

Willie Gillis: Package from Home by Norman Rockwell, 1941.

"To the garbage rack," he said. "Double quick." He thumbed Johnny Lisk and me to the back of the barracks.

At the garbage rack we found three extremely fragrant garbage cans. Outside, we found more. Lisk and I, citizen-soldiers, stared at them. The overcheerful private to whom we were assigned told us, "When you finish cleaning those, I want to be able to see my face in them!"

"There's no accounting for tastes," Lisk whispered. Nevertheless we cleaned them and polished them and left them spic and span.

"Now take 'em outside and paint 'em," said the private. "White. Git the black paint and paint 'HQCO—RRC' on both sides of all of them!"

"This is summer," I suggested. "Wouldn't something pastel look better?"

The sun was affecting the private. "I think you're right," he said. So we painted them cream and lettered them in brilliant orange.

All afternoon, in a blistering sun, we painted garbage cans. The other Charlotte boys waved to us as they passed on their way to the ballpark. Happy voices floated to us from the post exchange. The supper hour neared.

The straw-boss private woke up, yawned and went away, telling us what would happen if we did likewise. He returned soon on a truck. He motioned peremptorily to us and we loaded the cans into the truck. Away we went to headquarters company—and painted more garbage cans. It was definitely supper-time by now.

"Now can we go home, Private Dooley, sir?" asked Lisk. I looked at Lisk every time the blindness left me, and I could see the boy was tired.

The private sighed wearily. "Git in the truck," he said. Away we went back to our street. We stopped in front of our barracks and Private Dooley dismounted. "The truck driver," he said, "would appreciate it if you boys would go and help him wash the truck."

We sat in the back of the truck and watched the mess hall fade away behind us. Two, three, four miles we left it behind us. We had to wait ten minutes before we could get the wash pit. It took us fifteen minutes to wash the truck. By the time we got back to the mess hall, we were too tired to eat. But we ate.

"There's one thing to be thankful for," said Lisk. "Tomorrow can't be this bad."

On the way to our barracks we met Yardbird Fred McPhail, neat and cool, on his way to the recreation hall. "Good news, soldiers," said Yardbird McPhail. "We don't have to drill tomorrow."

We halted and sighed blissfully.

"No, sir," said McPhail. "They can't lay a hand on us from sunup until sundown. The whole barracks is on kitchen duty all day." ✶

Ack-Ack to Whistle-Jerk: Army Slang

Anonymous

*The put-downs of rank, bureaucracy, food, technology—every aspect of military life—
helped keep it all in perspective.*

ACK-ACK: Antiaircraft fire

ARMORED COW: Canned milk

ARMY BANJO: Shovel

BALLOON JUICE: Helium

BARRACKS LAWYER: Soldier who claims to be an
expert in regulations—and often finds
loop-holes for himself.

BATTERY ACID: Coffee

BITCH BOX: Loudspeaker. (Also "squawk box" in
the Navy.)

BLOOMER BOY: Paratrooper

BOBTAIL: Dishonorable discharge

BURP GUN: Machine gun

CAPTAIN OF THE HEAD: Idiot (*Navy*)

CHALK: Powdered milk

COVERED WAGON: Aircraft carrier (*Navy*)

CROW TRACKS: Chevrons

DOGFACE: GI

DOG SHOW: Foot inspection (*Army infantry*)

EAGLE DAY: Payday

FROGSTICKER: Bayonet

FRUIT SALAD: Award ribbons

FUBAR: shorthand for "F—up beyond all
recognition"

GOLD BRICK: Lazy person

GREMLIN: Mysterious mechanical problems.
  (*Coined by pilots in England.*)

HANG OUT THE LAUNDRY: Drop paratroopers

HOLY JOE: Chaplain

MAE WEST: Life vest

NINETY-DAY WONDER: Officer Candidate
  School graduate

PING JOCKEY: Radar operator

POOP: Official information

RACK TIME: Sleep (*Navy*)

RUPTURED DUCK: Honorable discharge insignia

SACK OUT: Sleep

SCRAMBLED EGGS: Gold braids of senior officers

SEAGULL: Canned chicken (*Navy*)

SEAWEED: Spinach (*Navy*)

SHAVETAIL: 2nd lieutenant

SNAFU: Shorthand for "Situation normal, all f—up."

V-GIRL: A woman who enthusiastically supports
  men in uniform

WHISTLE-JERK: Drill sergeant

From MISTER ROBERTS

THOMAS HEGGEN

Best remembered now as a classic film starring Henry Fonda and Jack Lemmon,
Mister Roberts *was first a best-selling novel and then a long-running Broadway play.*

TO A SUPERFICIAL OBSERVER, it might seem that there was a minimum of high, clear purpose to Ensign Pulver's life. A very close observer, scrutinizing Pulver under the lens, would reach the same conclusion. But if Pulver's direction was sometimes dubious, one thing was abundantly certain—that he would travel it in considerable contentment. Ensign Pulver was a quite happy and relaxed young man. He slept a great deal and very well, ate practically anything without complaint; and to any stimuli his reaction was apt to be remarkably amiable. He could and did absorb staggering amounts of well-intentioned insult, and his vanity appeared to be vulnerable on only one point: his feet. By accepted human standards, Ensign Pulver's feet were enormous, and he was delicate about them. He was apt to become abruptly dignified and not a little aloof when they were offered for discussion. They were offered frequently.

Ensign Pulver was a young man of a high degree of ingenuity. Most of this he directed toward his own well-being. Since foresight is the better part of ingenuity, he had reported aboard the ship burdened with a large and heavy wooden box. It would be fatuous to presume that this chest contained clothing. The three cases of beer, six quarts of bourbon, three of rum, one of gin, and two of Vermouth, had lasted, through admirable providence, almost six months, even though shared with Lieutenant Roberts and Ed Pauley and the Doc. Pulver had himself, over the objections of the other three, imposed the pace and the restraint. He had a predilection for certain things effete and sensuous, and he got a wonderful feeling of luxury from lying in his bunk sipping a beer or a Manhattan.

Young Pulver got to spending a lot of time in his bunk, asleep and awake. On an average day he probably spent eighteen hours in bed. He was an engineering officer. Although few of the officers had anything, really, to do, Pulver had less than most. It would be neither unfair nor very inaccurate to say that, professionally, he didn't do a thing. So he had a lot of time on his hands,

OPPOSITE:
Troop Ship Deck by James B. Turnbull, 1944.
Courtesy D. Wigmore Fine Art, Inc., NY.

186

and this, with his native ingenuity, he converted to time on his back. His bunk became to him a sort of shrine, and but for meals and other undeniable functions, he was seldom out of it. It was an unusually well-equipped bunk. At the foot Pulver had rigged a small fan which wafted cool breezes over him on the hottest nights. At the side was attached a coffee-can ash tray, a container for cigarettes and another for a lighter. Pulver liked to smoke in bed while he was reading. Books were stowed in the space between the springs and the bulkhead. Beer was kept there, too, and it was possible to open a bottle on the reading light on the bulkhead.

He read a great deal, being embarked upon an ambitious program of self-improvement. By education Pulver was a metallurgical engineer, and now read books that he had widely and willingly evaded during his college days. He read these books because they were the books that Lieutenant Roberts read; consciously or not, Ensign Pulver had set out to make himself over in Roberts's image. With regard to most objects, people, ideas, Pulver was languidly cynical; with a few he was languidly approving, and with almost none was he overtly enthusiastic. His admiration for Roberts was utterly unabashed. He thought that Roberts was the greatest guy he had ever known. He prodded him with questions on every conceivable subject, memorized the answers, then went back to his bunk and assiduously absorbed them into his own conversation. He watched the careless, easy dignity with which Roberts met the crew, and studied the way that Roberts got the crew to work for him; and then he tried to apply this dignity and this control to his own small authority. Being honest with himself, he couldn't notice any increased devotion in the eyes of the men; or indeed, anything more than the usual tolerance. It is not very likely that Ensign Pulver would ever have read Santayana, or the

English philosophers, or *Jean-Christophe*, or *The Magic Mountain*, if he had not seen Roberts reading them. Before this self-imposed apprenticeship, he had been content to stay within the philosophical implications of *God's Little Acre*. He had read *God's Little Acre* twelve times, and there were certain passages he could recite flawlessly.

His reading program didn't leave much time for anything else, but what leisure could be managed he devoted to planning characteristically ingenious actions against the Captain. He didn't really have cause for hard feeling against the Captain, because, being an engineer, he was quite remote from him. In truth, the Captain hardly knew Pulver was aboard. But because Roberts hated the Captain, Pulver felt duty-bound to do the same; and scarcely a day went by that he didn't present to Roberts the completed planning for a new offensive. To be sure, these offensives seldom went beyond the planning stage, because commonly their structure was so satisfying to Ensign Pulver that he felt fulfilled just in regarding it. Also he was not a very brave young man, and these things called for bravery just as surely as the battlefield.

Once he figured out a way to plug, far down in the sanitary system, the line that fed the Captain's head, so that the Captain would one day be deluged by a considerable backwash. He never did anything about it. He figured out a Rube Goldberg device that would punch the Captain in the face with a gloved fist when he entered his cabin. He never did anything about this either. Then he was going to introduce marbles into the overhead in the Captain's bedroom, the marbles to roll around at night and make an awful racket. He conferred frequently with the Doctor on ways of transmitting a gonococcus infection to the Captain. About the only plan he ever executed was one involving no personal risk. He did, one day while the

Captain was ashore, actually insert shavings from an electric razor into his bed, on the theory that they would serve as satisfactorily as any good itch powder. If they did, the evidences were disappointing, for although Pulver watched closely, the Captain never appeared better rested, and indeed, better-natured, than in the succeeding days.

One day, during a lull in his reading schedule, a wonderful idea for the Captain came to Pulver. It was one so stunning that he was able to recognize it immediately as his tour de force. It did not reveal itself to him gradually, as did most of his schemes, but instead it came with the sudden, inevitable force of predestination. It was, quite simply, tremendous: he would get some good substantial firecrackers and throw them into the Old Man's room at night. It was a wonderful idea, and yet it was so simple, so indicated, and so necessary, that Pulver marveled he hadn't thought of it before. The bastard would be walking on his heels for weeks afterward! What a splendid idea. Ensign Pulver dedicated several full minutes to self-congratulation.

After the first flush of creation, he permitted himself a little to be invaded by realism. He owned no firecrackers, he was sure there were none on the ship, and it was likely that the closest supply was at Honolulu, distant about two thousand miles. But such second-rate obstacles were no match for a thing predestined, and he easily surmounted them. Fireworks, he decided strongly, could be manufactured on the ship. Black powder, he thought, would do very nicely. He could make some kind of a fuse too. The idea was a natural—it couldn't possibly fail.

When the plan was complete and glowing in his mind, he took it, as he took all of his plans, to Lieutenant Roberts. This was quite late at night and Roberts had turned in. He wasn't very enthusiastic when he was awakened to hear the new plan: in fact, he was definitely hostile, if not to the plan, then at least to Pulver. He cursed Pulver vigorously. Then he turned over and went back to sleep.

Ensign Pulver was a little hurt at this reception, but it didn't diminish his faith in the plan one whit. He lay in his bunk that night and stayed awake an excessively long time, fifteen minutes or so, savoring the whole thing. The more he thought about it, the better it seemed. He went over in his mind just how it would be. He debated deliciously whether to attach a long time-fuse to the explosive, or to fix a short one, light it, throw it, and run like hell. He finally decided in favor of the short fuse as being the more exciting. He fell happily asleep, mesmerized by a vision of Captain Morton, pop-eyed with terror, quaking at the explosions that rocked his very sanity.

Next morning he was up at the unprecedented hour of nine. He went right to work. He found some good stout twine to use as a fuse. For a container he cut into firecracker lengths the cardboard roll of a clothes hanger. He went down to sick-bay and begged some potassium sulphate to saturate the fuse. Then he was ready for the explosive. Ensign Pulver was a competent metallurgist, but his knowledge of explosives was deficient. He had, in the course of the night, abandoned black powder as his choice and substituted fulminate of mercury. He knew that by repute fulminate of mercury was terrific stuff, and he reasoned that the best was none too good for this job. He went down to Olson, the gunner's mate, and obtained four primers used to detonate the old model five-inch bag ammunition. The primers contained fulminate of mercury.

He was ready then for the test. In a state of high excitement he hurried down to the

FOLLOWING PAGES:
On Deck by Richard Gibney, 1991.
U.S. Marine Corps Museum, Washington, D.C.

190

machine shop just aft of the engine room. The place was well chosen for its subterranean location, large cleared area, and corrugated steel deck. Ensign Pulver cut open the primers, sealed one end of a section of the cardboard tubing, filled the case with fulminate of mercury, inserted the potassium sulphate fuse and plugged the other end around it. He stood back then and viewed the product with an artist's pride. It bulged ominously and did not much resemble a firecracker. Ensign Pulver hummed and smiled happily as he found a match and lit the one-inch fuse.

He had made two miscalculations. They were fairly grave. He had underestimated the rate at which the potassium sulphate fuse would burn. It went like a streak. And he had grossly underestimated and completely misunderstood the explosive character of fulminate of mercury, which, particle for particle, is just about the most furious substance in the world. The signalmen, way up on the flying bridge, claimed that they could feel the explosion; and certainly every man on the ship heard it. The men in the engine room were terrified; they knew that finally a torpedo had struck. If the Captain had been aboard, he would almost certainly have been screaming, "Prepare to abandon ship!" It was quite a firecracker.

The Doc said that Ensign Pulver got off very light. His eyebrows and lashes were burned off, and the hair for an area of two inches back from his forehead. He received first-degree burns of the face, neck, and forearms. He was in sick-bay for a day soaking in tannic acid. After that he was up and around, but with his head and throat swathed like a mummy. Perhaps he was a proper object for sympathy, but his appearance short-circuited any that might have been forthcoming. He looked pretty silly without eyebrows and with his nose sticking out from the bandages like a beacon.

Just as a matter of policy Ensign Pulver always tried to avoid the Captain. He did pretty well, too, sometimes going two and three weeks without even seeing him. Now, however, just a few days after his accident, rounding a corner in the boat-deck passageway, he ran smack into Captain Morton. The Captain hadn't seen or heard of Pulver's condition, and his response was typically childlike. For a moment he gaped and goggled, and then he started chuckling. He had a particularly lewd and rasping chuckle, and he stood pointing at the turbaned Pulver and laughing like a child confronted by a clown.

"What the hell'd you do?" he demanded. "Stick your head in one of them goddam furnaces down there?" And he chuckled the more at his own wit.

Ensign Pulver forced a grin, said "Yessir," and started edging toward the down ladder.

The Captain looked at him benevolently. "Goddamn, boy," he chortled, "you want to keep your head out of those furnaces. Don't you know that?"

Pulver made another grin, said "Yessir" again sheepishly, and then, when he saw a chance only moderately rude, he ducked down the ladder. He was so furious he couldn't see straight. The goddamned smart-aleck, loud-mouthed son-of-a-bitch! He tried very hard to keep his anger focused on the Captain, but all the time he knew better. What really rubbed, he knew, was his conviction of the considerable justice in the Captain's laughter. ✴

into thinking I had permission to tag along with him. By the time we got back to the officers' club, I was so brave I was telling everybody the big things that Jack Austin and I were going to do.

The Colonel went outside and put in a phone call. When he came back he hauled me out of the crowd and said, "I've just talked to General Doolittle about you going on the mission tomorrow. He said to tell you to put down your glass and go to bed." This young Colonel, who looked like Clark Gable, drove me all the way back to Tunis in the headquarters car. As we got out in front of the hotel he said, "Get some sleep, dad." It aged me fifteen years, but I guess I had it coming to me. ★

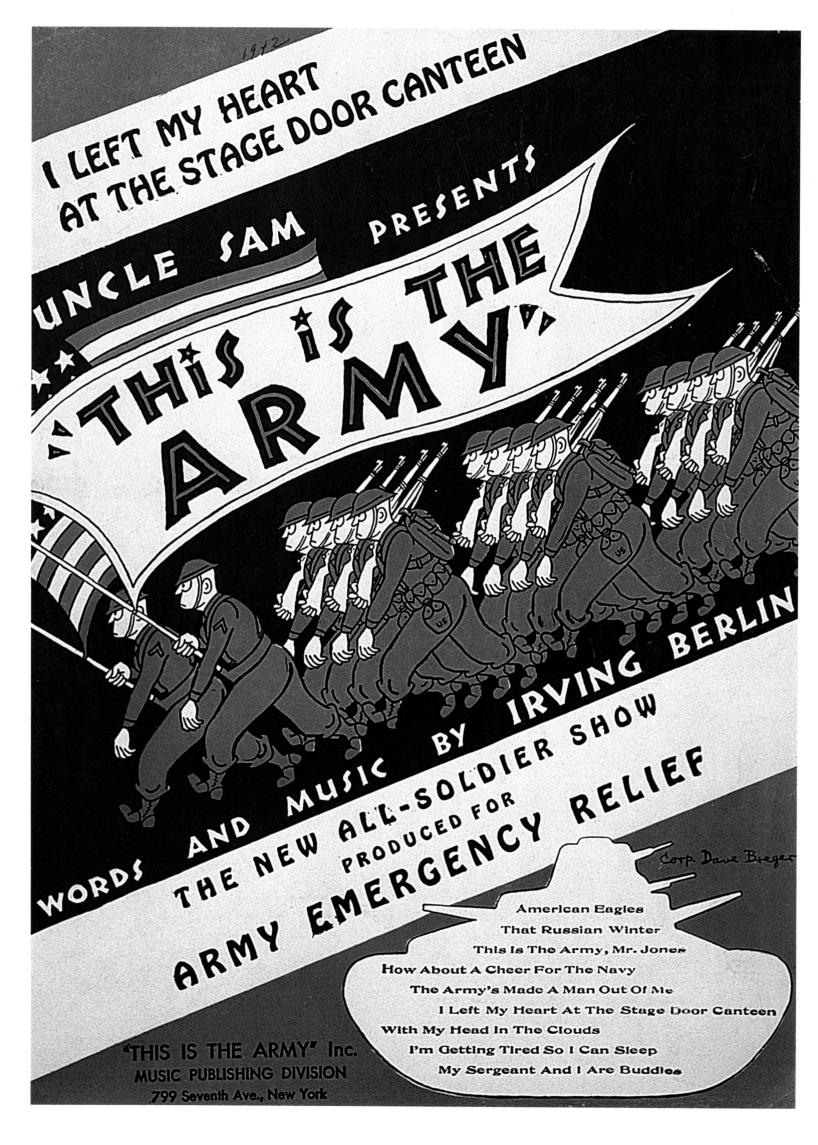

OUR SONGS

THIS IS THE ARMY, MISTER JONES

IRVING BERLIN

In the First World War, songwriter Irving Berlin amused both soldiers and civilians with "Oh How I Hate to Get Up in the Morning," written for a morale show called "Yip, Yip, Yaphank." (Yaphank was an army camp in New York.) For the Second World War he developed a new show called "This Is the Army," which toured the country to raise morale and sell war bonds. It was made into a movie starring Lt. Ronald Reagan.

A bunch of frightened rookies were list'ning filled with awe
They listened while a sergeant was laying down the law
They stood there at attention, their faces turning red
The sergeant looked them over and this is what he said:

This is the Army, Mister Jones
No private rooms or telephones
You had your breakfast in bed before
But you won't have it there any more

This is the Army, Mister Green
We like the barracks nice and clean
You had a housemaid to clean your floor
But she won't help you out any more

Do what the buglers command
They're in the Army and not in a band

This is the Army, Mister Brown
You and your baby went to town
She had you worried but this is war
And she won't worry you anymore

BOOGIE WOOGIE BUGLE BOY

DON RAYE AND HUGHIE PRINCE

The hits of LaVerne, Patty, and Maxene Andrews, including "Don't Sit Under the Apple Tree" and "Rum and Coca-Cola," were played nonstop during the war. The first female group to have a million-copy hit, the Andrews Sisters would eventually sell a staggering 90 million records. They also appeared in more than a dozen films, such as "In the Navy," "Buck Privates," "Follow the Boys," and "Hollywood Canteen."

He was a famous trumpet man
From old Chicago way
He had a boogie style
That no one else could play
He was the top man at his craft
But then his number came up
And he was gone with the draft
He's in the army now
A-blowin' reveille
He's the boogie woogie bugle boy of Company B

They made him blow a bugle
For his Uncle Sam
It really brought him down
Because he couldn't jam
The Captain seemed to understand
Because the next day the Cap'
Went out and drafted a band
And now the company jumps
When he plays reveille
He's the boogie woogie bugle boy of Company B

A-toot a-toot
A-toot diddle-ee-ada-toot
He blows it eight to the bar
In boogie rhythm
He can't blow a note
Unless the bass and guitar
Is playin' with 'im

He makes the company jump
When he plays reveille
He's the boogie woogie bugle boy of Company B

(THERE'LL BE BLUEBIRDS OVER) THE WHITE CLIFFS OF DOVER

NAT BURTON AND WALTER KENT

This melancholy standard became Vera Lynn's signature—and a constant reminder of Great Britain's resolute spirit.

There'll be bluebirds over
The white cliffs of Dover
Tomorrow, just you wait and see

There'll be love and laughter
And peace ever after
Tomorrow, when the world is free

The shepherd will tend his sheep
The valley will bloom again
And Jimmy will go to sleep
In his own little room again

There'll be bluebirds over
The white cliffs of Dover
Tomorrow, just you wait and see

FOLLOWING PAGES:
Canton Island—Pacific
by Paul Sample, 1943.

THE LIGHTER SIDE

The career of two-time Pulitzer Prize winner and best-selling author Bill Mauldin began at Stars and Stripes, where he created the infantry "dogfaces" Willie and Joe, and penned classic cartoons like the cavalry officer distraught at the loss of his Jeep. Sergeant George Baker's Sad Sack comic, which debuted in Yank magazine in 1942, lived on long after he war; it became a 1957 movie starring Jerry Lewis and was a regular comic book from 1949 to 1982. Howard Baer was a military artist and Esquire cartoonist. And every camp had at least one soldier like Sergeant Hooper, who lampooned army life in the post newsletter.

"Just gimme th' aspirin.
I already got a Purple Heart."

SGT. GEORGE BAKER

P.F.C. BAH! IT WASN'T LIKE THIS IN THE OLD ARMY.

"You told me to bring a friend!"

V-E Day on Wall Street, May 7th, 1945.

VII. LEGACY

"I know not with what weapons World War III will be fought, but World War IV will be fought with sticks and stones."

—ALBERT EINSTEIN

RETURNING HOME WAS NOT EASY. Having seen horrors they could not bring themselves to discuss, soldiers often felt isolated from their families and other civilians. Many men felt uncomfortable when treated as heroes, because they believed simply being alive disqualified them from that honor. Petty office politics seemed even more ridiculous than army life.

And suddenly everything was upside down: The Germans were friends. The Russians, without whom defeat of the Nazis would have been impossible (and who suffered the worst casualties of any of the European Allies) were the new enemy. The same held true in Asia: Japan was our new best friend; China, once the beneficiary of our support, became an adversary after its Communist revolution. Meanwhile, at home, many women had tasted independence and were not willing to relinquish it.

There was also the matter of the 15-kiloton punctuation mark dropped at the end of the war, an event that stirred much debate. President Harry Truman was thought by many to be callous in deciding to use it, despite having given the question serious thought. In any case, the mere existence of the bomb was overwhelming and left the future unclear. But its symbolic power was even greater than its destructive force. The knowledge that the next world war might be the last proved an effective deterrent during several moments of crisis in the decades that followed.

As in every war, the conflict never ended for an unfortunate few. James Bradley's father helped raise the American flag at Iwo Jima; that event would hound him and the other flag raisers for the rest of their lives. Poets Robert Graves and James Tate were stuck in time for even deeper reasons.

We also seem to be stuck in time. The Second World War continues to dominate the minds of authors and filmmakers, who insist on examining this huge experience from every angle. At any hour one can find a war documentary on television. Yet the panoramic newsreel scenes tell only part of the story. There is something essential about the war that can only be understood through the feelings of the men and women who experienced it.

OPPOSITE:
The Enola Gay at Hiroshima
by Robert Andrew Parker, 2000.

HIROSHIMA

After Germany surrendered in May 1945, Japan continued to fight. The Allies, advancing through the Pacific from island to island, readied themselves for an invasion of Japan similar to the D-Day invasion of Europe. But a secret project in the New Mexico desert succeeded in developing an atomic bomb, promising a quicker end to the war with fewer casualties. In August 1945, A-bombs were dropped on Hiroshima and Nagasaki, forcing Japan's surrender.

From

MEMOIRS OF HARRY S. TRUMAN: YEAR OF DECISIONS

HARRY S TRUMAN

I HAD REALIZED, of course, that an atomic bomb explosion would inflict damage and casualties beyond imagination. On the other hand, the scientific advisers of the committee reported, "We can propose no technical demonstration likely to bring an end to the war; we see no acceptable alternative to direct military use." It was their conclusion that no technical demonstration they might propose, such as over a deserted island, would be likely to bring the war to an end. It had to be used against an enemy target.

The final decision of where and when to use the atomic bomb was up to me. Let there be no mistake about it. I regarded the bomb as a military weapon and never had

any doubt that it should be used. The top military advisers to the President recommended its use, and when I talked to Churchill he unhesitatingly told me that he favored the use of the atomic bomb if it might aid to end the war.

In deciding to use this bomb I wanted to make sure that it would be used as a weapon of war in the manner prescribed by the laws of war. That meant that I wanted it dropped on a military target. I had told Stimson that the bomb should be dropped as nearly as possible upon a war production center of prime military importance.... Four cities were finally recommended as targets: Hiroshima, Kokura, Niigata, and Nagasaki.... ✶

Detail from *Garden at Hiroshima*
by Standish Backus, 1946.

From

THE WORLD AT WAR

PAUL TIBBETS

THE DAY WAS CLEAR when we dropped that bomb, it was a clear sunshiny day and the visibility was unrestricted. As we came back around again facing the direction of Hiroshima we saw this cloud coming up. The cloud by this time, now two minutes old, was up at our altitude. We were 33,000 feet at this time and the cloud was up there and continuing to go right on up in a boiling fashion, as if it was rolling and boiling. The surface was nothing but a black boiling, like a barrel of tar. Where before there had been a city with distinctive houses, buildings and everything that you could see from our altitude, now you couldn't see anything except a black boiling debris down below. ✱

From

HIROSHIMA

JOHN HERSEY

THE REVEREND MR. TANIMOTO got up at five o'clock that morning. He was alone in the parsonage, because for some time his wife had been commuting with their year-old baby to spend nights with a friend in Ushida, a suburb to the north. Of all the important cities of Japan, only two, Kyoto and Hiroshima, had not been visited in strength by *B-san*, or Mr. B, as the Japanese, with a mixture of respect and unhappy familiarity, called the B-29; and Mr. Tanimoto, like all his neighbors and friends, was almost sick with anxiety. He had heard uncomfortably detailed accounts of mass raids on Kure, Iwakuni, Tokuyama, and other nearby towns; he was sure Hiroshima's turn would come soon. He had slept badly the night before, because there had been several air-raid warnings. Hiroshima had been getting such warnings almost every night for weeks,

FOLLOWING PAGES:
Settlers in New Hiroshima
by Standish Backus, 1946.

for at that time the B-29s were using Lake Biwa, northeast of Hiroshima, as a rendezvous point, and no matter what city the Americans planned to hit, the Superfortresses streamed in over the coast near Hiroshima. The frequency of the warnings and the continued abstinence of Mr. B with respect to Hiroshima had made its citizens jittery; a rumor was going around that the Americans were saving something special for the city.

Mr. Tanimoto was a small man, quick to talk, laugh, and cry. He wore his black hair parted in the middle and rather long; the prominence of the frontal bones just above his eyebrows and the smallness of his mustache, mouth, and chin gave him a strange, old-young look, boyish and yet wise, weak and yet fiery. He moved nervously and fast, but with a restraint which suggested that he was a cautious, thoughtful man. He showed, indeed, just those qualities in the uneasy days before the bomb fell. Besides having his wife spend the nights in Ushida, Mr. Tanimoto had been carrying all the portable things from his church, in the close-packed residential district called Nagaragawa, to a house that belonged to a rayon manufacturer in Koi, two miles from the center of town. The rayon man, a Mr. Matsui, had opened his then unoccupied estate to a large number of his friends and acquaintances, so that they might evacuate whatever they wished to a safe distance from the probable target area. Mr. Tanimoto had had no difficulty in moving chairs, hymnals, Bibles, altar gear, and church records by pushcart himself, but the organ console and an upright piano required some aid. A friend of his named Matsuo had, the day before, helped him get the piano out to Koi; in return, he had promised this day to assist Mr. Matsuo in hauling out a daughter's belongings. That is why he had risen so early.

Mr. Tanimoto cooked his own breakfast. He felt awfully tired. The effort of moving the piano the day before, a sleepless night, weeks of worry and unbalanced diet, the cares of his parish—all combined to make him feel hardly adequate to the new day's work. There was another thing, too: Mr. Tanimoto had studied theology at Emory College, in Atlanta, Georgia; he had graduated in 1940; he spoke excellent English; he dressed in American clothes; he had corresponded with many American friends right up to the time the war began; and among a people obsessed with a fear of being spied upon—perhaps almost obsessed himself—he found himself growing increasingly uneasy. The police had questioned him several times, and just a few days before, he had heard that an influential acquaintance, a Mr. Tanaka, a retired officer of the Toyo Kisen Kaisha steamship line, an anti-Christian, a man famous in Hiroshima for his showy philanthropies and notorious for his personal tyrannies, had been telling people that Tanimoto should not be trusted. In compensation, to show himself publicly a good Japanese, Mr. Tanimoto had taken on the chairmanship of his local *tonarigumi*, or Neighborhood Association, and to his other duties and concerns this position had added the business of organizing air-raid defense for about twenty families.

Before six o'clock that morning, Mr. Tanimoto started for Mr. Matsuo's house. There he found that their burden was to be a *tansu*, a large Japanese cabinet, full of clothing and household goods. The two men set out. The morning was perfectly clear and so warm that the day promised to be uncomfortable. A few minutes after they started, the air-raid siren went off—a minute-long blast that warned of approaching planes but indicated to the people of Hiroshima only a slight degree of danger, since it sounded every morning at this time, when an American weather plane came over. The two men pulled and pushed the handcart through the city streets. Hiroshima was a fan-shaped city, lying mostly on the six islands formed by the seven estuarial rivers that branch out from the Ota River; its main commercial and residential districts, covering about four square miles in the center of the city, contained three-quarters of its population, which had been reduced by several evacuation programs from a wartime peak of 380,000 to about 245,000. Factories and other residential districts, or suburbs, lay compactly around the edges of the city. To the south were the docks, an airport, and the island-studded Inland Sea. A rim of mountains runs around the other three sides of the delta. Mr. Tanimoto and Mr. Matsuo took their way through the shopping center, already full of people, and across two of the rivers to the sloping streets of Koi, and up them to the outskirts and foothills. As they started up a valley away from the tight-ranked houses, the all-clear sounded. (The Japanese radar operators, detecting only three planes, supposed that they comprised a reconnaissance.) Pushing the handcart up to the rayon man's house was tiring, and the men, after they had maneuvered their load into the driveway and to the front steps, paused to rest awhile. They stood with a wing of the house between them and the city. Like most homes in this part of Japan, the house consisted of a wooden frame and wooden walls supporting a heavy tile roof. Its front hall, packed with rolls of bedding and clothing, looked like a cool cave full of fat cushions. Opposite the house, to the right of the front door, there was a large, finicky rock garden. There was no sound of planes. The morning was still; the place was cool and pleasant.

Then a tremendous flash of light cut across the sky. Mr. Tanimoto has a distinct recollection that it travelled from east to west, from the city toward the hills. It seemed a sheet of sun. Both he and Mr. Matsuo reacted in terror—and both had time to react (for they were 3,500 yards, or two miles, from the center of the explosion). Mr. Matsuo dashed up the front steps into the house and dived among the bedrolls and buried himself there. Mr. Tanimoto took four or five steps and threw himself between two big rocks in the garden. He bellied up very hard against one of them. As his face was against the stone, he did not see what happened. He felt a sudden pressure, and then splinters and pieces of board and fragments of tile fell on him. He heard no roar. (Almost no one in Hiroshima recalls hearing any noise of the bomb. But a fisherman in his sampan on the Inland Sea near Tsuzu, the man with whom Mr. Tanimoto's mother-in-law and sister-in-law were living, saw the flash and heard a tremendous explosion; he was nearly twenty miles from Hiroshima, but the thunder was greater than when the B-29s hit Iwakuni, only five miles away.)

When he dared, Mr. Tanimoto raised his head and saw that the rayon man's house had collapsed. He thought a bomb had fallen directly on it. Such clouds of dust had risen that there was a sort of twilight around. In panic, not thinking for the moment of Mr. Matsuo under the ruins, he dashed out into the street. He noticed as he ran that the concrete wall of the estate had fallen over—toward the house rather than away from it. In the street, the first thing he saw was a squad of soldiers who had been burrowing into the hillside opposite, making one of the thousands of dugouts in which the Japanese apparently intended to resist invasion, hill by hill, life for life; the soldiers were coming out of the hole, where they should have been safe, and blood was running from their heads, chests, and backs. They were silent and dazed.

Under what seemed to be a local dust cloud, the day grew darker and darker. ✶

THE WAR GOD

STEPHEN SPENDER

Why cannot the one good Benevolent feasible
Final dove descend?

And the wheat be divided?
And the soldiers sent home?
And the barriers torn down?
And the enemies forgiven?
And there be no retribution?

Because the conqueror
Is an instrument of power,
With merciless heart hammered
Out of former fear,
When today's vanquished
Destroyed his noble father,
Filling his cradle with anguish.

His irremediable victory
Chokes back sobbing anxiety
Lest children of the slain
(When the ripe ears grow high
To the sickles of his own
And the sun goes down)
Rise in iron morning
To stain with blood the sky
And avenge their fathers again.

His heart broke before
His raging splendour.
The virgins of prayer
Fumble vainly for that day
Buried under ruins,
Of his pride's greatest murder
When his heart which was a child
Asking and tender,
He hunted and killed.

The lost filled with lead
On the helpless field
May dream the pious
Of mercy, but also
Their eyes know what they did
In their own proud season,
Their dead teeth bite the earth
With semen of new hatred.

For the world is the world
And not the slain
Nor the slayer, forgive,
Nor do wild shores
Of passionate histories
Close on endless love;
Though hidden under seas
Of chafing despair,
Love's need does not cease.

Infantry, Near Nijmegen, Holland by Captain David (Alex) Colville, 1945–46. Canadian War Museum, Ottawa.

PEGGY TERRY

from *The Good War*

STUDS TERKEL

---

*The acclaimed reporter and oral historian Terkel interviewed Terry
for his oral history of the Second World War. The notes are his.*

SHE IS A MOUNTAIN WOMAN WHO HAS LIVED IN CHICAGO FOR THE PAST TWENTY YEARS. PADUCAH, KENTUCKY, IS HER HOMETOWN. SHE VISITS IT AS OFTEN AS HER MEAGER PURSE ALLOWS.

THE FIRST WORK I HAD after the Depression was at a shell-loading plant in Viola, Kentucky. It is between Paducah and Mayfield. They were large shells: anti-aircraft, incendiaries, and tracers. We painted red on the tips of the tracers. My mother, my sister, and myself worked there. Each of us worked a different shift because we had little ones at home. We made the fabulous sum of thirty-two dollars a week. (Laughs.) To us it was just an absolute miracle. Before that, we made nothing.

You won't believe how incredibly ignorant I was. I knew vaguely that a war had started, but I had no idea what it meant.

DIDN'T YOU HAVE A RADIO?

Gosh, no. That was an absolute luxury. We were just moving around, working wherever we could find work. I was eighteen. My husband was nineteen. We were living day to day. When you are involved in stayin' alive, you don't think about big things like a war. It didn't occur to us that we were making these shells to kill people. It never entered my head.

There were no women foremen where we worked. We were just a bunch of hillbilly women laughin' and talkin'. It was like a social. Now we'd have money to buy shoes and a dress and pay rent and get some food on the table. We were just happy to have work.

I worked in building number 11. I pulled a lot of gadgets on a machine. The shell slid under and powder went into it. Another lever you pulled tamped it down. Then it moved on a conveyer belt to another building where the detonator was dropped in. You did this over and over.

Tetryl was one of the ingredients and it turned us orange. Just as orange as an orange. Our hair was streaked orange. Our hands, our face, our neck just turned orange, even our eyeballs. We never questioned. None of us ever asked, What is this? Is this harmful? We simply didn't think about it. That was just one of the conditions of the job. The only thing we worried about was other women thinking we had dyed our hair. Back then it was a disgrace if you dyed your hair. We worried what people would say.

We used to laugh about it on the bus. It eventually wore off. But I seem to remember some of the women had breathing problems.

OPPOSITE:
Home Front by Jolan Gross-Bettelheim, 1942–43.

The shells were painted a dark gray. When the paint didn't come out smooth, we had to take rags wet with some kind of remover and wash that paint off. The fumes from these rags—it was like breathing cleaning fluid. It burned the nose and throat. Oh, it was difficult to breathe. I remember that.

Nothing ever blew up, but I remember the building where they dropped in the detonator. These detonators are little black things about the size of a thumb. This terrible thunderstorm came and all the lights went out. Somebody knocked a box of detonators off on the floor. Here we were in the pitch dark. Somebody was screaming, "Don't move, anybody!" They were afraid you'd step on the detonator. We were down on our hands and knees crawling out of that building in the storm. (Laughs.) We were in slow motion. If we'd stepped on one . . .

Mamma was what they call terminated—fired. Mamma's mother took sick and died and Mamma asked for time off and they told her no. Mamma said, "Well, I'm gonna be with my mamma. If I have to give up my job, I will just have to." So they terminated Mamma. That's when I started gettin' nasty. I didn't take as much baloney and pushing around as I had taken. I told 'em I was gonna quit, and they told me if I quit they would blacklist me wherever I would go. They had my fingerprints and all that. I guess it was just bluff, because I did get other work.

I think of how little we knew of human rights, union rights. We knew Daddy had been a hell-raiser in the mine workers' union, but at that point it hadn't rubbed off on any of us women. Coca-Cola and Dr. Pepper were allowed in every building, but not a drop of water. You could only get a drink of water if you went to the cafeteria, which was about two city blocks away. Of course you couldn't leave your machine long enough to go get a drink. I drank Coke and Dr. Pepper and I hated 'em. I hate 'em today. We had to buy it,

of course. We couldn't leave to go to the bathroom, 'cause it was way the heck over there.

We were awarded the Navy E for excellence. We were just so proud of that E. It was like we were a big family, and we hugged and kissed each other. They had the Navy band out there celebrating us. We were so proud of ourselves.

First time my mother ever worked at anything except in the fields—first real job Mamma ever had. It was a big break in everybody's life. Once, Mamma woke up in the middle of the night to go to the bathroom and she saw the bus going down. She said, "Oh my goodness, I've overslept." She jerked her clothes on, threw her lunch in the bag, and was out on the corner, ready to go, when Boy Blue, our driver, said, "Honey, this is the wrong shift." Mamma wasn't supposed to be there until six in the morning. She never lived that down. She would have enjoyed telling you that.

My world was really very small. When we came from Oklahoma to Paducah, that was like a journey to the center of the earth. It was during the Depression and you did good having bus fare to get across town. The war just widened my world. Especially after I came up to Michigan.

My grandfather went up to Jackson, Michigan, after he retired from the railroad. He wrote back and told us we could make twice as much in the war plants in Jackson. We did. We made ninety dollars a week. We did some kind of testing for airplane radios.

Ohh, I met all those wonderful Polacks. They were the first people I'd ever known that were any different from me. A whole new world just opened up. I learned to drink beer like crazy with 'em. They were all very union-conscious. I learned a lot of things that I didn't even know existed.

We were very patriotic and we understood that the Nazis were someone who would have to be stopped. We didn't know

Victory Sparks by Howard Baer, 1943.

about concentration camps. I don't think anybody I knew did. With the Japanese, that was a whole different thing. We were just ready to wipe them out. They sure as heck didn't look like us. They were yellow little creatures that smiled when they bombed our boys. I remember someone in Paducah got up this idea of burning everything they had that was Japanese. I had this little ceramic cat and I said, "I don't care, I am not burning it." They had this big bonfire and people came and brought what they had that was made in Japan. Threw it on the bonfire. I hid my cat. It's on the shelf in my bathroom right now. (Laughs.)

In all the movies we saw, the Germans were always tall and handsome. There'd be one meanie, a little short dumpy bad Nazi. But the main characters were good-lookin'

and they looked like us. The Japanese were all evil. If you can go half your life and not recognize how you're being manipulated, that is sad and kinda scary.

I do remember a nice movie, *The White Cliffs of Dover*. We all sat there with tears pouring down our face. All my life, I hated England, 'cause all my family all my life had wanted England out of Ireland. During the war, all those ill feelings just seemed to go away. It took a war.

I believe the war was the beginning of my seeing things. You just can't stay uninvolved and not knowing when such a momentous thing is happening. It's just little things that start happening and you put one piece with another. Suddenly, a puzzle begins to take shape. ✷

A GHOST FROM ARAKAN

ROBERT GRAVES

---

*This poem was written in 1956. Graves's son, David, died
in combat on Burma's Arakan coast, in 1943.*

He was not killed. The dream surprise
Sets tears of joy pricking your eyes.
    So cheated, you awake:
A castigation to accept
After twelve years in which you've kept
    Dry-eyed, for honour's sake.

His ghost, be sure, is watching here
To count each liberated tear
    And smile a crooked smile:
Still proud, still only twenty-four,
Stranded in his green jungle-war
    That's lasted all this while.

Ghost Trail by Kerr Eby, 1944.

Dive Bombing Japanese Carriers at Midway by Griffith Bailey Coale, 1942.

IN SOME DRAWER...

from *James Jones: A Friendship*

WILLIE MORRIS

ONE WINTER NIGHT Jim and [his son] Jamie and I were sitting around the kitchen table talking. We had been discussing something about the war. Jamie asked: "Why haven't you ever showed me your medals, Dad?"

"Because I don't believe in that shit," Jim said.

"Where are they?"

"Tucked away in some drawer in the attic, I guess."

"Well, I'd like to see them."

Reluctantly he trudged upstairs and rummaged for a while. Jamie and I heard the thud of big objects from the floors above. Then he came back with a box. He sat down at the table and brought out an

assortment of ribbons and medals and blew the dust off them. Jamie wanted to know what each one was.

"This here's Good Conduct. They took that one away once and then give it back . . . .This is for Guadalcanal." An orange-and-red-striped one was the Asiatic-Pacific campaign ribbon and medal, with a bronze star on it for Midway. Another was the yellow American Defense ribbon, with a battle star, he said, for Pearl Harbor.

"What's this pretty one?"

"That's the Bronze Star."

"And this one?"

"That there's the Purple Heart. But this one here, it's the only one we wore when we shipped home." He pointed to the replica of a rifle on a field of blue with a silver wreath around it. "It's the Combat Infantryman's Badge."

"Why is it the only one you ever wore?"

"Oh, shit, I don't know. It was a point of pride, you see—better than all the rest. It spoke for itself. It really meant something. It was just an unspoken rule. If you wore any of the others, the men would've laughed you out of town, or maybe whipped your ass." ★

FOLLOWING PAGES:
Score Another for the Subs
by Thomas Hart Benton, 1943.

From

FLAGS OF OUR FATHERS

JAMES BRADLEY WITH RON POWERS

Bradley's father, John, was one of the men who raised the flag on Iwo Jima's Mount Suribachi. That event was captured in a photograph that became, for the three flagraisers who survived the battle for the island, unbearably significant.

ONE OF MY DAD'S FINER QUALITIES was simplicity.

He lived by simple values, values his children could understand and emulate.

He had no hidden agendas; he expressed himself directly. He had a knack for breaking things down into quiet, irreducible truths.

"It's as simple as that," he'd say. "Simple as that."

BUT A FLAGRAISER'S EXISTENCE wasn't always so simple.

In 1979, the Chicago *Tribune* writer Mary Elson was following up on [fellow flagraiser] Rene [Gagnon]'s death and surprised John Bradley at his desk at the McCandless, Zobel & Bradley Funeral Home.

He gave her about "ten agitated minutes of his time," puffing "nervously on a cigarette . . . sitting on the edge of his chair in the electric pose of a runner ready to bolt from a starting block."

He spent most of those ten minutes downplaying the perceived heroics of the flagraising. But in two of his sentences he revealed his thinking about that eternal 1/400th of a second. "You think of that pipe. If it was being put in the ground for any

other reason . . . Just because there was a flag on it, that made the difference."

Here my father captured the two competing realities of The Photograph. It was an action of common virtue, not uncommon valor, as plain as a pipe. . . .

OR MAYBE IT WAS SOMETHING ELSE. Something too painful to reopen. In 1964, when he was forty and I was nine, my father hinted at why he couldn't talk about Iwo Jima. But I was too young to really understand.

My third-grade class was studying American history. When we got to World War II, there, on page 98 of our textbook, was The Photograph.

My teacher told the class that my father was a hero. I was proud as only a young son can be.

That afternoon I sat near the back door of our house with my history book open to page 98, waiting for Dad to come home from work. When he finally walked through the door, I jumped toward him before he'd even had a chance to take off his coat.

"Dad!" I exclaimed. "Look! There's your picture! My teacher says you're a hero and

Poster, United States Marine Corps, 1945. U.S. Marine Corps Museum, Washington, D.C.

she wants you to speak to my class. Will you give a speech?"

My father didn't answer me right away. He closed the door and walked me gently over to the kitchen table. He sat down across from me. He took my textbook and looked at The Photograph. Then he gently closed the book.

After a moment he said, "I can't talk to your class. I've forgotten everything."

That was often his excuse, that he couldn't remember.

But then he went on: "Jim, your teacher said something about heroes."...

I shifted expectantly in my chair. I thought now I would hear some juicy stories of valor. Instead, he looked me directly in my nine-year-old eyes signaling that he'd like to embed an idea in my brain for the rest of my life.

Then he said: "I want you to always remember something. The heroes of Iwo Jima are the guys who didn't come back."

Simple as that. ✱

THE
LOST PILOT

JAMES TATE

[FOR MY FATHER, 1922–1944]

Your face did not rot
like the others—the co-pilot,
for example, I saw him

yesterday. His face is corn-
mush: his wife and daughter,
the poor ignorant people, stare

as if he will compose soon.
He was more wronged than Job.
But your face did not rot

like the others—it grew dark,
and hard like ebony;
the features progressed in their

distinction. If I could cajole
you to come back for an evening,
down from your compulsive

orbiting, I would touch you,
read your face as Dallas,
your hoodlum gunner, now,

with the blistered eyes, reads
his braille editions. I would
touch your face as a disinterested

scholar touches an original page.
However frightening, I would
discover you, and I would not

turn you in; I would not make
you face your wife, or Dallas,
or the co-pilot, Jim. You

could return to your crazy
orbiting, and I would not try
to fully understand what

it means to you. All I know
is this: when I see you,
as I have seen you at least

once every year of my life,
spin across the wilds of the sky
like a tiny, African god,

I feel dead. I feel as if I were
the residue of a stranger's life,
that I should pursue you.

My head cocked toward the sky,
I cannot get off the ground,
and, you, passing over again,

fast, perfect, and unwilling
to tell me that you are doing
well, or that it was a mistake

that placed you in that world,
and me in this; or that misfortune
placed these worlds in us.

I SHOOK HER HAND

from Barry Broadfoot's
Six War Years: 1939–1945

ANONYMOUS

I DON'T KNOW IF EVERYBODY expected us to be only 85 pounds and be wearing rags, but when we came to Canada they treated us like we were in cotton batting. They meant well, and I guess it was right that we should be grateful. Think of it, not everybody had spent one-sixth of their life in a Japanese prison camp. I was twenty when Hong Kong was captured and I was twenty-four when we got home.

Everything was a blur. I mean that. We didn't eat much but potato soup with some fish in it, but we stole more than our share of rice, and the Americans who first had us looked after us pretty well, so when I got home, I was in pretty fair shape. Except I was very nervous and I would cry sometimes over little things, and I didn't know what was happening. Canada was a changed place. The people were different, it seemed.

I remember coming home on the train. I don't know if we were the first Grenadiers to come home but they treated us pretty good and some reporters and photographers got on

our coach at Brandon and rode with us to Winnipeg and it was one long string of asking questions and taking pictures and I was afraid. I don't know why, but I didn't say anything. Then this photographer came back and he said he'd done something wrong with his camera and he'd like to take another picture and I broke down and started to cry. The photographer looked like a nice guy and it was smoothed over.

Then we got into Winnipeg, the station across from the Fort Garry. I used to play in the old fort in the park there when I was a kid. I'd joined up when I was nineteen. I think there were lots of people in the station. Maybe the mayor, for all I know.

What I should be telling you now, if I can, is that I had a wife too, but I didn't know what she looked like. I mean I wasn't sure. The Japs had taken away our wallets and things and when I got mine back, or maybe it was my paybook, her picture was gone. Her name was Mary. We'd had a few dates. I couldn't afford much. We'd go bowling, five pins, and then have a Denver sandwich, and then I'd walk her to her boarding house and that would be it. Three

Detail from *Union Station, Chicago, 1944*
by Norman Rockwell, 1944.

weeks before I went to Hong Kong we got married, and I was afraid I wouldn't know what she looked like. I don't think my brain was working all that well.

I guess I should say that I didn't really know her. Hadn't heard from her, you see. We got no mail. A couple of guys did, but the Japs always seemed to lose mine.

I can't remember much about the station. Maybe there was a ceremony. There were a lot of people moving around and then, just like that, I hear this voice say, "Hello, Johnny." I turn around and there she is, and it's not the girl I thought it would be, because I honestly couldn't remember. It was all a blur.

You know what I did? I'm not kidding. I shook her hand. Like that, I shook her hand. She was a little thing.

I remember her saying, "C'mon, Johnny, we're going home. Have you got your bag?" and I had a little bag and I picked it up and walked out. It was October. The sun was shining. I remember that. About eleven in the morning. I could stretch this out and tell you other things, but all I remember is, I was crying and a taxi guy jumps out and opens the door and we get in. I couldn't remember if I'd been in a taxi in the past four or five years, but if I had I guess it was in Victoria or Vancouver. Wherever we landed. I can't, I don't think I can remember.

It was just a short trip, a few blocks. She just held my hand, and I must have just held hers and wiped my eyes with the other, with a hankie, and then we got out at the Garrick Hotel. I don't know if it is still there, but it was a funny little place. Little but tall, and we got out and she said, "Here's home for now, Johnny," and I got out and I remember when we were walking up the first flight of stairs the taxi driver comes charging up and he's got my bag. I'd left it. There was nothing

in it anyway. I had nothing, just army stuff. Not even a gift. When he got to us he held out the bag to Mary and he squeezed my arm, right here where the muscle is, and he said, "Everything's gonna be fine. You wait and see." I'll always remember that guy.

We got to the room, just an ordinary hotel room in an ordinary hotel, you might say. It wasn't even a good room. A 2-dollar room, I'd say. I did some dumb things, like going to the dusty window and making knots-and-crosses in the dust, playing a game with myself. I asked her how her dad was and she said fine. I think I wasn't crying any more. Hell, this was 30 years ago. How can I remember everything?

I sat down on the bed and she went to her bag and brought out a bottle of Johnny Walker Red Label. Never forget it. She held it up and said, "You're home, Johnny. Johnny's home," and I got up and hugged her. That was the first time. I think, honestly, that that was when she just started to get through to me. That she just wasn't some little girl who had picked me up in the station.

I said we weren't altogether right. We looked okay, 150 pounds, new haircut, new uniforms, the medals we'd earned, and I guess I had about 3,000 bucks back pay coming and enough for a start, but we weren't right. We weren't right emotionally. We weren't ready for our wives. Know that?

I poured myself a drink and one for Mary and another and another and in about an hour we had finished the bottle. I mean I had. She had a couple, maybe three. Then I took off my tunic and lay down on the bed and zonk, that was it. Out. Before I went under I saw Mary taking off her blouse and her little skirt and she lay down beside me and she held me.

That was the start of my coming back to the world. I can't put it any other way. It took a long time and I was terrified a lot, but that was the start and that was it. The start. ★

WWII Timeline

1931

September 18th: Japan invades Manchuria in northeast China, later creating the puppet state of Manchukuo. It already controls Korea, and plans further Asian colonies.

1933

January 30th: Adolf Hitler is appointed Chancellor of Germany.
March 4th: FDR is inaugurated as President of the U.S.
March 23rd: The Dachau concentration camp receives its first prisoners.
March 27th: Japan withdraws from the League of Nations.
October 14th: Germany withdraws from the League of Nations.

1935

March 16th: Germany announces its intention to rearm, contrary to the Versailles Treaty that ended the First World War.
August 31st: U.S. passes Neutrality Act, restricting support of any warring countries. This act will be strengthened by another such act on May 1, 1937.
October 3rd: Italy, a Fascist power, invades Ethiopia, which falls in May, 1936.

1936

March 7th: Germany, defying the Versailles Treaty, sends troops into the Rhineland.
July 17th: Civil War erupts in Spain.
October 1st: Francisco Franco leads the Fascist rebellion.
November 26th: Germany and Japan sign the Anti-Comintern Pact to stop Soviet activities abroad.

1937

November 5th: In meeting with military leaders, Hitler makes clear his plan to expand Germany's borders and "preserve" the German "race" through war.
December 13th: Japanese troops capture China's capital, Nanking. A grotesque massacre follows in which 300,000 Chinese are killed.

1938

March 12th: Germany forces union with Austria.
October 1st: German troops occupy the Sudetenland area of Czechoslovakia after it was ceded to Germany at the Munich Conference the day before.

1939

March 15th: Germany takes the remainder of Czechoslovakia.
March 28th: Madrid falls to Franco's forces; Spanish Civil War ends with Fascist victory.
May 22th: Germany and Italy make pact.
August 12th: Albert Einstein writes to FDR to suggest the possibility of an atomic bomb.
September 1st: Germany invades Poland.
September 3–10th: Britain, France, Canada, Australia, and New Zealand declare war on Germany.
August 23rd: Germany and U.S.S.R. make "non-aggression" pact, and secretly divide Europe into proposed territories.
September 5th: U.S. declares its neutrality.
September 17th: U.S.S.R. invades Poland.

1940

April 9th: Germany invades Denmark and Norway.
May 10th: Germany invades France, Netherlands, Belgium, and Luxembourg. British Prime Minister Neville Chamberlain resigns. Winston Churchill selected to replace him.
May 12th: Germans begin Blitzkrieg across France.
May 26–June 4th: Evacuation of British, French, and Belgian troops from Dunkirk.
June 12th: British Army in North Africa attacks Italian forces.
June 14th: German troops enter Paris. France officially falls June 22nd.
July 10th: Battle of Britain air war begins.
September 16th: In prelude to the draft, U.S. Congress passes act requiring registration for military service.
September 27th: Japan, Germany, and Italy sign the Tripartite Pact, formalizing the Axis.

1941

March 11th: U.S. begins Lend-Lease program, so called because Allies were lent money to be spent on war equipment from U.S. manufacturers. (Approximately $49 billion would be eventually offered, primarily to Britain, China, and the U.S.S.R.)

May 24–27th: In major battles of the Atlantic war, Germany's *Bismarck* sinks the Royal Navy's *Hood*, then is chased and sunk by the Royal Navy's *Ark Royal* and others.

June 22nd: Thinking western Europe secure, Germany invades sometimes ally U.S.S.R. to begin war on second front.

July 26th: U.S. suspends relations with Japan, and siezes its assets.

December 7th: Japanese make surprise attack on Hawaii; at the same time they attack the Philippines, Wake Island, Guam, Malaya, Thailand, Shanghai, and Midway, and invade Malaya and Thailand.

December 8th: U.S. and Britain declare war on Japan.

December 11th: Germany and Italy declare war on U.S.

December 10–18th: Japanese forces invade the Philippines, Guam, Burma, Borneo, and Hong Kong.

1942

March 2nd: Internment of 120,000 Americans of Japanese descent begins; Canada will also intern Canadians of Japanese descent.

April 9th: U.S. forces on Bataan in Philippines surrender to Japanese; Bataan Death March, in which 76,000 troops are forced to march to POW camp, begins next day—20,000 will die.

June 4–5th: Crucial victory for Allies as the Japanese fleet is defeated near Midway Island.

August 7th: Allies begin the first offensive in their island-hopping operations with invasion of Tulagi and Guadalcanal.

August 1942–February 1943: Soviets successfully resist Germans at Stalingrad.

November 12th: American and British forces invade North Africa.

1943

May 13th: In what is largely a tank war, the Allies defeat Axis forces in North Africa.

July 9th: From secured bases in North Africa, Allies land on Sicily, then invade mainland Italy.

September 8th: Italy surrenders. Allies begin push northward to Germany and occupied France.

November 20th: U.S. Marines and Army troops invade Tarawa and Makin Islands, opening the American offensive in the Central Pacific.

1944

June 6th: D-Day, the Allied invasion of Occupied France. Hundreds of thousands of troops land on northern coast of France to press Germans back into the Allied troops advancing from Italy.

August 25th: Paris is liberated.

October 23–26th: In the Pacific, the Battle of Leyte Gulf effectively destroys the Japanese fleet; this battle sees the first use of kamikaze ("divine wind") suicide attacks.

December 16th: Last-ditch German offensive, the Battle of the Bulge, leaves Allied troops surrounded until relieved by Third Army troops led by General George Patton.

1945

January 28th: German forces eliminated from the Bulge.

February 21st: U.S. troops recapture Bataan in the Philippines.

March 16th: The island of Iwo Jima is captured.

April 29th: Allied troops liberate Dachau concentration camp.

April 30th: With Allied troops advancing toward his fortress, Hitler commits suicide.

May 7th: Germany surrenders.

June 9th: Japanese government announces intention to fight to the death rather than surrender to Allies.

August 6th and 9th: Atomic bombs dropped on Hiroshima and Nagasaki.

August 14th: Japan agrees to armistice; surrenders unconditionally on September 2nd.

Time-Life Books is a division of Time Life Inc.
Time-Life is a trademark of Time Warner Inc. and affiliated companies.

TIME LIFE INC.

Chairman and Chief Executive Officer Jim Nelson
President and Chief Operating Officer Steven Janas
Senior Executive Vice President and Chief Operating Officer Mary Davis Holt
Senior Vice President and Chief Financial Officer Christopher Hearing

TIME-LIFE BOOKS

President Larry Jellen
Senior Vice President, New Markets Bridget Boel
Vice President, Home and Hearth Markets Nicholas M. DiMarco
Vice President, Content Development Jennifer L. Pearce

TIME-LIFE TRADE PUBLISHING

Vice President and Publisher Neil S. Levin
Senior Sales Director Richard J. Vreeland
Director, Marketing and Publicity Inger Forland
Director of Trade Sales Dana Hobson
Director of Custom Publishing John Lalor
Director of Rights Licensing Olga Vezeris

WWII

New Product Development Manager Lori A. Woehrle
Executive Editor Linda Bellamy
Director of Design Tina Taylor
Project Manager Jennifer L. Ward
Director of Production Carolyn Bounds

PRODUCED BY FAIR STREET PRODUCTIONS AND WELCOME ENTERPRISES, INC.

Project Directors Susan Wechsler, Lena Tabori
Project Editor Susan Wechsler
Project Manager Natasha Tabori Fried
Art Director Gregory Wakabayashi
Photo Researcher Sherri Zuckerman/Photosearch, Inc.
Traffic Coordinator Shaie Dively/Photosearch, Inc.

School and library distribution by Time-Life Education, P. O. Box 85026, Richmond, Virginia 23285-5026.

Library of Congress Cataloging-in-Publication Data

WWII : a tribute in art and literature / edited by David Colbert.
   p.   cm.
  ISBN 0-7370-3146-6 (hardcover)
  1. World War, 1939–1945–Literary collections. 2. World War, 1939–1945–Art and the
war. 3. American literature–20th century. 4. English literature–20th century. I. Title:
WW2. II. Title: World War II. III. Colbert, David.

PS509.W66 W88 2001
810.8'0358–dc21

2001023694

Printed in Singapore
10 9 8 7 6 5 4 3 2 1

LITERARY CREDITS

Langston Hughes, "The Underground" from *Collected Poems of Langston Hughes*. Copyright ©1994 by The Estate of Langston Hughes. Used by permission of Alfred A. Knopf, a division of Random House, Inc.

Walter Lord, "The Little Ships" from *The Miracle of Dunkirk*, by Walter Lord. Copyright © 1982 by Walter Lord. Used by permission of Viking Penguin, a division of Penguin Putnam, Inc.

James Jones, excerpt from *From Here to Eternity*. Copyright ©1951 James Jones. Copyright renewed 1979 by Gloria Jones, James Phillipe Jones, and Kaylie Anne Jones. Used by permission of Dell Publishing, a division of Random House, Inc.

William Faulkner, "Two Soldiers," from *Collected Stories of William Faulkner*, by William Faulkner. Copyright © 1942, and renewed 1970 by Estelle Faulkner & Jill Faulkner Summers. Used by permission of Random House, Inc.

James A. Michener, "The Airstrip at Konora," from *Tales of the South Pacific*, by James A. Michener. Copyright © 1946, 1947 by Curtis Publishing Company. Copyright © 1947 by James A. Michener, copyright renewed © 1975 by James A. Michener. Reprinted with the permission of Scribner, a division of Simon & Schuster, Inc.

Marge Piercy, "Bernice 2, Bernice on Patrol," excerpt from *Gone to Soldiers*, by Marge Piercy. Copyright © 1987 by Middlemarsh, Inc. Reprinted with the permission of Simon & Schuster, Inc.

Henry Reed, "Naming of Parts" from "Lessons of the War," from *Collected Poems*, by Henry Reed, edited by Jon Stallworthy (1991). Reprinted by permission of Oxford University Press.

Nell Giles, "Rosie the Riveter," excerpt from *Punch In, Susie! A Woman's War Factory Journal*. Copyright 1943 by Nell Giles. Copyright renewed ©1971 by Nell Giles Ahern. Reprinted by permission of HarperCollins Publishers, Inc.

James Gould Cozzens, excerpt from *Guard of Honor*, by James Gould Cozzens. Copyright ©1948 and renewed 1975 by James Gould Cozzens, reprinted by permission of Harcourt, Inc.

Louis MacNeice, "Swing-song," from *Collected Poems*, November 1942, by Louis MacNeice. Reprinted with acknowledgment to publishers, Faber & Faber, Ltd., and the Literary Executors of the Louis MacNeice Estate, David Higham Associates, Ltd.

William Chappell, from "The Sky Makes Me Hate It" Copyright © William Chappell.

Lincoln Kirsten, "Rank." Copyright ©1966 by the New York Public Library (Astor, Lenox and Tilden Foundations). Not to be reproduced without permission.

John Steinbeck, "Magic Pieces" and "Superstition," from *Once There Was a War*, by John Steinbeck. Copyright © 1943, 1958 by John Steinbeck. Renewed © 1971 by Elaine Steinbeck, John Steinbeck IV, and Thomas Steinbeck. Used by permission of Viking Penguin, a division of Penguin Putnam Inc.

James Dickey, "The Island," from *The Whole Motion: Collected Poems, 1945–1992*, by James Dickey. Copyright © 1992 by James Dickey and reprinted by permission of Wesleyan University Press.

Anonymous, "Leaving Home," from *Six War Years: 1939–1945*, by Barry Broadfoot. Copyright © 1974 by Barry Broadfoot. Used by permission of Doubleday, a division of Random House, Inc.

Dylan Thomas, "A Refusal to Mourn the Death, by Fire, of a Child in London," from *The Poems of Dylan Thomas*. Copyright © 1945 by The Trustees for the Copyrights of Dylan Thomas. Reprinted by permission of New Directions Publishing Corp. and the Literary Executors of the Dylan Thomas Estate, David Higham Associates, Ltd.

William L. White, excerpt from *They Were Expendable*. Copyright © 1942 and renewed 1970 by W. L. White, reprinted by permission of Harcourt, Inc.

Joy Kogawa, from *Obasan*, reprinted with the permission of the author. First published in 1981 by Lester & Orpen Dennys and by Penguin Canada in 1983.

© John M. Bennett, "Who's Afraid of the New Focke-Wulf?"

Len Deighton, from *Bomber*. Copyright © 1970, Len Deighton, Pluriform Publishing Company BV. Reprinted by kind permission of Jonathan Clowes Ltd., London, on behalf of Pluriform Publishing Company BV.

Daniel K. Inouye, "Go for Broke," from *Journey to Washington*, by Senator Daniel K. Inouye with Lawrence Elliot. Copyright © 1967 by Prentice Hall, Inc., copyright renewed 1995 by Senator Daniel K. Inouye. Reprinted with the permission of Simon & Schuster, Inc.

Irwin Shaw, from *The Young Lions*. © Irwin Shaw. Reprinted with permission. All rights reserved. Published by the University of Chicago Press.

Herbert Read, "To a Conscript of 1940," from *Collected Poems*, by Herbert Read. Reprinted with acknowledgment to publishers, Faber & Faber, Ltd., and the Literary Executors of the Herbert Read Estate, David Higham Associates, Ltd.

Czeslaw Milosz, "The Opaque Had Become Transparent," from *Native Realm*, by Czeslaw Milosz, translated by Catherine S. Leach. Copyright © 1968 by Doubleday, a division of Bantam Doubleday Dell Publishing Group, Inc. Used by permission of Doubleday, a division of Random House, Inc.

Thomas Keneally, from *Schindler's List*, by Thomas Keneally. Copyright © 1982 by Hemisphere Publishers Ltd. Reprinted with permission of Simon & Schuster, Inc.

Primo Levi, from *If This Is a Man (Survival in Auschwitz)*, translated by Stuart Woolf. Copyright © 1959 by Orion Press, Inc. © 1958 by Giulio Einaudi editore S. P. A. Used by permission of Viking Penguin, a division of Penguin Putnam Inc.

Roy Fuller, "What Is Terrible," from *Collected Poems*, by Roy Fuller. Copyright © John Fuller, André Deutsch Ltd. Used by permission of John Fuller, 4 Benson Place, Oxford OX2 6QHR.

Walter McDonald, "Digging in a Footlocker," from *Counting Survivors*, by Walter McDonald. Copyright © 1995. Reprinted by permission of the University of Pittsburgh Press.

R. N. Currey, "Unseen Fire," from *This Other Planet*, by R. N. Currey. © 1945 London: Routledge.

ART CREDITS

The editors would like to thank all the archives, institutions, collectors, and individuals who so graciously provided us with information and images, especially: Renée Klish and Kevin Prude at the U.S. Army Center of Military History; Anne-Marie Ehrlich at The Art Archive, London; Leslie Redman at the Canadian War Museum; Dilip Banerjee at the Imperial War Museum, London; Gail Monroe, Karin Haubold, and Frank Arre at the Navy Art Collection, Naval Historical Center.

Page 6: Christie's Images, NY

Page 8: Army Art Collection, U.S. Army Center of Military History

Page 11: Courtesy George M. Harding, Jr. and Anita Kistler

Page 13: National Archives and Records Administration

Pages 14–15: Gift of Marvin Small, 1948. Courtesy Jacob & Gwendolyn Lawrence Foundation

Page 22: Courtesy Martin Jacobs, Mjacobs784@aol.com

Page 24: Navy Art Collection, Naval Historical Center

Page 27: The Art Archive, London

Pages 30–31: Navy Art Collection, Naval Historical Center

Page 35: National Archives and Records Administration

Page 37: Army Art Collection, U.S. Army Center of Military History

Page 38: Courtesy George M. Harding, Jr. and Anita Kistler

Pages 40–41: AWM ART27628

Page 45: AAAC889/290 (Archives New Zealand Head Office, Wellington, NZ)

Page 46: Library of Congress

Page 50: All, National Archives and Records Adminstration

Page 51: All, National Archives and Records Administration, except bottom right, Library of Congress

Page 52: National Archives and Records Administration

Page 57: National Archives and Records Administration

Pages 58–59: The Art Archive, London.

Page 60: Art Resource, NY

Pages 62–63: Navy Art Collection, Naval Historical Center

Page 64: Army Art Collection, U.S. Army Center of Military History

Page 67: Army Art Collection, U.S. Army Center of Military History

Pages 68–69: Navy Art Collection, Naval Historical Center, Gift of Abbott Laboratories

Pages 70–71: Navy Art Collection, Naval Historical Center, Gift of Abbott Laboratories

Page 72: © Canadian War Museum , C.W.M. catalog no. 10592

Page 75: Navy Art Collection, Naval Historical Center

Pages 76–77: Navy Art Collection, Naval Historical Center

Page 78: National Archives and Records Administration

Pages 86–87: AWM ART27632

Page 89: Gift of Madeleine Sugimoto and Naomi Tagawa (92.97.3)

Pages 92–93: Army Art Collection, U.S. Army Center of Military History

Pages 96–97: United States Air Force Art Collection

Page 100: Army Art Collection, U.S. Army Center of Military History

Page 103: Navy Art Collection, Naval Historical Center

Page 104: © Canadian War Museum, C.W.M. catalog no. 12657

Page 106: Navy Art Collection, Naval Historical Center

Pages 108–09: Navy Art Collection, Naval Historical Center

Page 111: Navy Art Collection, Naval Historical Center

Page 112: AAAC898/74 (Archives New Zealand Head Office, Wellington, NZ)

Page 115: National Archives and Records Administration

Pages 116–17: U.S. Army Center of Military History

Page 119: © Auguste Moses-Nussbaum and Shulamit Jaari

Page 120: Photo courtesy Simon Wiesenthal Center Library and Archives, Los Angeles, CA

Page 128: Navy Art Collection, Naval Historical Center

Page 131: Navy Art Collection, Naval Historical Center

Page 133: Egg tempera on composition board, 20 x 16 inc. (50.8 x 40.6 cm.), Collection of Whitney Museum of American Art, Gift of Mr. and Mrs. Roy R. Neuberger, 51.19. Courtesy Jacob & Gwendolyn Lawrence Foundation. Photo: Geoffrey Clements

Page 139: © Canadian War Museum C.W.M. catalog no. 83198

Page 140: Captain George W. Rarey, KIA June 27, 1944. http://www.rareybird/com

Page 144: Army Art Collection, U.S. Army Center of Military History

Page 146: Army Art Collection, U.S. Army Center of Military History

Pages 148–49: Navy Art Collection, Naval Historical Center

Pages 150–51: Navy Art Collection, Naval Historical Center

Page 153: Army Art Collection, U.S. Army Center of Military History

Page 154: The Art Archive, London

Page 158: National Archives and Records Administration

Page 161: Navy Art Collection, Naval Historical Center

Page 162: A.W.M. ART24352

Pages 164–65: Navy Art Collection, Naval Historical Center

Page 167: © Canadian War Museum, C.W.M. catalog no. 12172

Page 168: Photo courtesy The Royal Collection ©2001, Her Majesty Queen Elizabeth II. Photo: Prudence Cumming

Pages 170–71: © Canadian War Museum, C.W.M. catalog no. 12296

Page 173: Army Art Collection, U.S. Army Center of Military History

Page 176: Courtesy Tracy Sugarman, the author and illustrator of *My War: A Love Story in Letters and Drawings*, Random House, Inc., 2000

Page 177 top: Courtesy Jennifer and Peter Sanfilippo

Page 177 bottom: Captain George W. Rarey, KIA June 27, 1944. http://www.rareybird/com

Page 179: National Archives and Records Administration

Page 181: Printed by permission of the Norman Rockwell Family Trust. Copyright © 2001 the Norman Rockwell Family Trust, courtesy Curtis Publishing Co.

Page 182: Originally published in *Camp Davis AA Barrage*

Page 183: Originally published in *Camp Davis AA Barrage*

Page 192: Courtesy Military Antiques & Museum, Petaluma, CA. warstuff@sonic.net

Page 193: Fair Street Pictures

Pages 194–95: Army Art Collection, U.S. Army Center of Military History

Page 196: Courtesy Lester Glassner Collection. Photo: Brownie Harris

Page 198: Courtesy Lester Glassner Collection. Photo: Brownie Harris

Page 199: Photofest

Pages 200–01: Army Art Collection, U.S. Army Center of Military History

Pages 202–03 top: "The Sad Sack: Spam," by Sgt. George Baker, c. 1944

Page 203 center: "The Sad Sack: Objective," by Sgt. George Baker, c. 1944

Page 203 lower left: Originally published in *Hawaii Brief*

Page 203 lower right: From "One World is Enough," by Howard Baer. By permission of *Esquire* magazine, © Hearst Communications, Inc. *Esquire* is a trademark of Hearst Magazines Property, Inc. All Rights Reserved

Page 204: © Corbis

Pages 208–09: Navy Art Collection, Naval Historical Center

Pages 210–11: Navy Art Collection, Naval Historical Center

Pages 214–15: © Canadian War Museum, C.W.M. catalog no. 12172

Page 216: Library of Congress

Page 219: Navy Art Collection, Naval Historical Center

Pages 220–21: Navy Art Collection, Naval Historical Center

Pages 222–23: Navy Art Collection, Naval Historical Center

Pages 224–25: Navy Art Collection, Naval Historical Center, Gift of Abbot Laboratories

Page 228: Navy Art Collection, Naval Historical Center

Pages 230–31: Printed by permission of the Norman Rockwell Family Trust. Copyright © 2001 the Norman Rockwell Family Trust, courtesy Curtis Publishing Co.

Page 232: Library of Congress

The Nuremberg Trial by Dame Laura Knight, 1943. Imperial War Museum, London.

ACKNOWLEDGMENTS

Susan Wechsler and the team at Fair Street Productions and Gregory Wakabayashi at Welcome Enterprises selected the art in this book. Greg's design elevated both the art and the text.

Susan, along with Jennifer Ward and Linda Bellamy of Time Life, offered editorial guidance for which I am grateful.

Others at Time Life were also essential to this book's creation, especially Jennifer Pearce, Robert Somerville, Inger Forland, and Tina Taylor.

Lena Tabori and Natasha Tabori Fried of Welcome made it possible for me to be involved with this project.

Kevin Mahoney's detailed fact-checking was most helpful.

I'd also like to thank my father, a WWII veteran (AAF), for his excellent suggestions of text contributors.

—DAVID COLBERT